COMP...
f...
ANIM...

COMPASSION
for
ANIMALS

Readings and Prayers

Edited by
ANDREW LINZEY
and
TOM REGAN

First published in Great Britain 1988
SPCK
Holy Trinity Church
Marylebone Road
London NW1 4DU

British Library Cataloguing in Publication Data

Compassion for animals.
   1. Animals. Treatment by man.
   Ethical aspects. Christian viewpoints
   I. Linzey, Andrew, 1952–   II. Regan, Tom
   241'.693

ISBN 0-281-04352-3

Printed in Great Britain by
Hazell Watson & Viney Limited
Member of BPCC plc
Aylesbury, Bucks

To
Arthur Broome
1780–1837

An Anglican priest who founded the Society for the Prevention of Cruelty to Animals, the first animal welfare society in the world, serving as its first secretary, suffering imprisonment for the Society's debts, and dying in obscurity. Long may his name be honoured among those who work for the cause of animals.

The royalties from the first printing of this work sold in the United Kingdom will be given to the Royal Society for the Prevention of Cruelty to Animals and in the United States to the Culture and Animals Foundation.

THE REVD DR ANDREW LINZEY is Chaplain and Director of Studies of the Centre for the Study of Theology in the University of Essex. He is author of *Animal Rights: A Christian Assessment* (SCM Press 1976); *The Status of Animals in the Christian Tradition* (Woodbrooke College, Birmingham 1985); and *Christianity and the Rights of Animals* (SPCK 1987). He is editor (with Peter J. Wexler) of *Heaven and Earth: Essex Essays in Theology and Ethics* (Churchman 1986) and (with Tom Regan) of *Animals and Christianity: A Book of Readings*, SPCK 1988. For four years he was a member of the National Council of the RSPCA.

PROFESSOR TOM REGAN is Professor of Philosophy at the North Carolina State University and President of the Culture and Animals Foundation. He is author or editor of over twenty books including *Animal Sacrifices* (Temple University Press 1986) and *All That Dwell Therein* (University of California Press 1983). His *Case for Animal Rights* (University of California Press 1984) is the definitive work on the subject. He has also directed a film on religious attitudes to animals entitled *We are all Noah*.

Contents

Acknowledgements

We are indebted, like our predecessors, to those who have collected and quarried before us. In particular we would like to acknowledge our indebtedness to the late Ambrose Agius's work *God's Animals* (London, Catholic Study Circle for Animal Welfare, 1970); the late C. W. Hume's *The Status of Animals in the Christian Religion* (London, Universities Federation for Animal Welfare, 1957); and Richard Newman's *Bless All Thy Creatures, Lord: Prayers for Animals* (London and New York, Macmillan, 1982), all of which provided useful material or pointed us in the right directions. Our greatest thanks must go to Jon Wynne-Tyson's *The Extended Circle: A Dictionary of Humane Thought* (Fontwell, Sussex, Centaur Press, 1985) which has already established itself as a classic in this field and which has been an indispensable quarry in producing this collection.

We are grateful to Penelope Fleming and Nicholas Garrard at Westcott House, Cambridge, for their help in researching this book.

The Scripture quotations in this publication are from the Revised Standard Version of the Bible, copyrighted 1946, 1952, © 1971, 1973 by the Division of Christian Education of the National Council of the Churches of Christ in the USA, and are used by permission.

We are grateful to the following for permission to reproduce copyright material:

Collins Publishers for the quotation from Tertullian taken

from Bro. Kenneth CGA (ed.), *From the Fathers to the Church*, the prayer by St Francis from G. and M. Harcourt (eds), *Short Prayers for the Long Day*, and the extract from P. Teilhard de Chardin, *Hymn of the Universe*.

Faber and Faber Ltd for the poem 'Anthem' by W. H. Auden, and Faber and Faber Ltd and Harcourt Brace Jovanovich for the extract from T. S. Eliot, *Murder in the Cathedral*.

David Higham Associates Ltd for the extract from the poem 'Still Falls the Rain' by Edith Sitwell.

Macmillan Ltd for 'The Prayer of the Dog' by Carmen Bernos de Gasztold.

John Murray (Publishers) Ltd and Cartal and Graf for the extract from Axel Munthe, *The Story of San Michele*.

Oxford University Press for the prayer by George Appleton from Appleton (ed.), *The Oxford Book of Prayer*, and the extract from St Athanasius, *Contra Gentile and De Incarnatione*, ed. and tr. R. W. Thomson.

SCM Press for the extracts from John Calvin, *Commentaries*, tr. J. Haroutunian and from J. Moltmann, *God in Creation*.

Sphere/Abacus for the extract from E. F. Schumacher, *Small is Beautiful*.

Unwin Hyman Ltd for the extracts from Albert Schweitzer, *My Life and Thought* and *Civilization and Ethics*.

For complete publication details, see 'Notes on Sources'. The publishers have made every effort to trace and acknowledge copyright holders of the material included in this anthology. Information on any omissions should be communicated to the publishers, who will make full acknowledgement in future editions of the book.

Foreword

by Cindy Milburn

Head of Education, RSPCA

I see this collection as instrumental in putting compassion for animals back on the human agenda. Richard Martin, a founder member of the RSPCA, felt that one of the Society's major tasks was to alter the moral feeling of the country. With recent statistics indicating that cruelty to animals is at an all-time high in Britain, that task is more pressing now than ever. Richard Martin and the early supporters of the Society – people like William Wilberforce and Lord Shaftesbury – would surely have warmly approved of this book.

Education in compassion has always been central to the work of the RSPCA. Our aim is not just to prevent cruelty but also to promote kindness. Andrew Linzey and Tom Regan have produced a book which powerfully supports that aim, making available a rich collection of readings and prayers that will encourage many of us to reflect more deeply on our attitudes to our fellow creatures. This is a book for use in our homes and our schools as well as our churches. On behalf of the humane movement, I congratulate Andrew and Tom on their achievement.

Human beings are a species under threat – largely from themselves. We injure, exploit and destroy on a massive scale. If we are to pass out of history we seem determined to take all other life with us. It is therefore in our own interest to change our attitudes and behaviour towards the natural world. If we do not, the survival of all species, including our own, is in jeopardy. 'Not until we extend the circle of compassion to include all living things,' wrote Albert Schweitzer, 'shall we ourselves know peace.' This book will help extend that circle.

Preaching the Gospel to Every Creature

Love all God's creation, the whole of it and every grain of sand. Love every leaf, every ray of God's light! Love the animals, love the plants, love everything. If you love everything, you will perceive the divine mystery in things. And once you have perceived it, you will begin to comprehend it ceaselessly more and more every day. And you will at last come to love the whole world with an abiding, universal love. Love the animals: God has given them the rudiments of thought and untroubled joy. Do not, therefore, trouble it, do not torture them, do not deprive them of their joy, do not go against God's intent. Man, do not exalt yourself above the animals: they are without sin, while you with your majesty defile the earth by your appearance on it and you leave the traces of your defilement behind you – alas, this is true of almost every one of us!

Dostoevsky's fine and powerful words go to the very heart of the gospel. For the divine mystery is nothing less than the love of God which sustains and energizes the whole universe. This inexhaustible source, deep and fathomless, encompasses all created beings. 'All things were made through him, and without him was not anything made that was made,' writes St John. Every creature is a loved creature – or it is no creature at all. The self-giving, sacrificial love of Christ is nothing less than the showing forth, the making flesh, of this sheer, incomprehensible generosity which is the indestructible grace of God.

And yet this is not a truth simply to be wondered at, as we may wonder at the myriads of stars or the breathtaking beauty of a sunset. It is, as Dostoevsky explains, something that must be lived. We have to love *in order to perceive*, and in perceiving come close to comprehension. For 'once you have perceived it, you will begin to comprehend it ceaselessly more and more every day'. Only a loving, forgiving, generous heart can put us right with God; everything else is of no avail. No systems, dogmas, creeds, priests, institutions or structures can save us if we are mean, unloving, unfeeling people. And this compassion must extend, if it is to be real, to the whole world of fellow creatures. Christian love cannot exclude animals. 'God', writes Dostoevsky, 'has given them the rudiments of thought and untroubled joy.' Moreover animals, despite the fallenness of creation, are innocent in ways which we cannot know: 'they are without sin, while you with your majesty defile the earth by your appearance on it'.

It is easy to mock (as doubtless we have all done on one or more occasions in our lives) at the figure of 'gentle Jesus, meek and mild'; and yet there is great strength in gentleness, heroism in forbearance, and power in humility. If Jesus can wash the dirty feet of our world, then surely his followers should heal the wounds of those suffering non-human creatures with whom we are to share this good earth. 'What is a charitable heart?' asks St Isaac the Syrian. 'It is a heart', he replies, 'which is burning with love for the whole creation, for men, for the birds, for the beasts, for the demons – for all creatures. He who has such a heart cannot see or call to mind a creature without his eyes being filled with tears by reason of the immense compassion which seizes his heart; a heart which is softened and can no longer bear to see or learn from others of any suffering, even the smallest pain, being inflicted upon a creature.'

This compassionate, sensitive heart for animals is inseparable from the proclamation of the Christian Gospel. We have lived so long with the Gospel stories of Jesus that we frequently fail to see how his life and ministry identified with animals at almost every point. His birth, if tradition is to be believed, takes place in the home of sheep and oxen. His ministry begins, according to St Mark, in the wilderness 'with the wild beasts' (1.13). His triumphal entry into Jerusalem involves riding on a 'humble' ass (see Matthew 21.1b–5). According to Jesus it is lawful to 'do good' on the Sabbath, which includes the rescuing of an animal fallen into a pit (see Matthew 12.10b–12). Even the sparrows, literally sold for a few pennies in his day, are not 'forgotten before God'. God's providence extends to the entire created order, and the glory of Solomon and all his works cannot be compared to that of lilies of the field (Luke 12.27). God so cares for his creation that even 'foxes have holes, and birds of the air have nests; but the Son of man has nowhere to lay his head' (Luke 9.58). It is 'the merciful' who are 'blessed' in God's sight and what we do to 'the least' of all we do to him (Matthew 5.7 and 25.45–6).

Moreover, what many commentators have failed to realize is that Jesus literally overturns the already questioned practice of animal sacrifice. Those who sell pigeons have their tables overturned and are put out of the Temple (Mark 11.15–16). It is the scribe who sees the spiritual bankruptcy of the animal sacrifice and the supremacy of sacrificial love that Jesus commends as being 'not far from the Kingdom of God' (see Mark 12.32–4). It is a loving heart which is required by God, and not the needless bloodletting of God's creatures. We can see the same prophetic and radical challenge to tradition in Jesus' remarks about the '*good* shepherd' who, unlike many in his day, '*lays down his life for the sheep*' (John 10.11, emphasis added). A line which, according to Robin Attfield, 'must have influenced its readers' attitudes to actual flocks as well as to the pastoral care of Christ for his followers'.[1] Even in the heavily gnostic Gospel of Thomas, there is the striking saying about the birds of the air and the fishes of the sea perhaps even preceding us in the Kingdom.[2] Whatever the authenticity of the saying, it seems strangely in keeping with the Spirit of Jesus.

In all this Jesus represents the best of the Jewish tradition expressed in that rabbinical saying that 'the way a person treats an animal is an index to his soul'. For it is a 'righteous man' who 'has regard for the life of his beast, but the mercy of the wicked is cruel' (Proverbs 12.10). Hence all the various humane prescriptions in the law of Moses about caring for animals and even the story of Balaam's ass, however bizarre it may appear to us today, is early testimony to the spiritual capacities of beasts (see Numbers 22.21–33). Indeed the Old Testament is unequivocal about the spiritual status of animals, for they too possess, according to Genesis, the 'breath of life' (see 1.30–1) so that 'when thou takest away their breath, they die and return to their dust' (see Psalm 104.27–31). Perhaps it is for this reason that Psalm 36 can confidently proclaim that 'man and beast thou savest, O Lord' (36.6b) which is surely a sign of that fundamental closeness between man and animals expressed in the important notion of covenant. For it is not only with

Noah and his descendants but also with 'every living creature' that the covenant is made (see Genesis 9.8–17).

If we ask why it is that so many Old Testament writers had this sense of the value and worth of creation, the answer must lie in the emerging doctrine of God the loving Creator of all. For animals are made with man on the same day in the order of creation, and are also similarly blessed (see Genesis 1.24–8). God the free, generous Creator puts man in the garden of Eden 'to till it and keep it'; that is, to exercise lordship over animals but under God's moral rule. Alas, man does not live up to God's expectations and it is not long before the Lord 'was sorry that he had made man' because of all the violence upon the earth (see Genesis 6.5–13). It is simply not true that God gave man a free hand to do what he liked with creation. On the contrary, made in the image of God man has a duty to reflect, if not actualize, the divine love for all creatures.

Perhaps it is for this reason that we find so many biblical passages speaking of the hope of a better, more peaceful world in which humans live in harmony with other creatures. Despite their sense of being involved in and responsible for the violence and carnivorousness of the world, the Hebrews never gave up their hope of cosmic redemption. 'I will make for you a covenant on that day with the beasts of the field, and I will abolish the bow, the sword, and war from the land,' says the Lord (see Hosea 2.18). The vision of Isaiah, where the wolf lies down with the lamb and the lion with the calf, and where 'they shall not hurt or destroy in all my holy mountain' (see Isaiah 11.6–9) haunted their moral consciences, aware as they were that the world, though good, is not yet as it should be.

Christians, too, as they came to reflect upon the nature of the love of God expressed in his Son Jesus Christ, began to see that the will of God was inclusive of all things. 'For he has made known to us in all wisdom and insight the mystery of his will, according to his purpose which he set forth in Christ as a plan for the fullness of time,' writes St Paul, 'to unite all things in him, things in heaven and things on earth' (Ephesians 1.9–10). Christ the supreme example of God's love was also seen to be the agent of cosmic peace and reconciliation. 'For in him all the fullness of God was pleased to dwell, and through him to reconcile to himself all things, whether on earth or in heaven, making peace by the blood of his cross' (see Colossians 1.19–20). This staggering conception of the cosmic Christ, healing the pain of creation and overcoming all division, is surely one of the most profound theological ideas in the New Testament. It finds further confirmation in St Paul's graphic portrayal of creation as groaning in childbirth, awaiting 'the glorious liberty of the children of God' (see Romans 8.18–23). Although the creation now suffers, and suffers abundantly, it shall not always be so. As humans are themselves renewed by the Spirit of Christ, so shall creation itself be renewed, indeed it will find a new freedom as God originally intended.

When we turn to the saints we find, almost without exception, a prefiguring of this lost world of cosmic peace. Again, we know so well the picturesque stories of St Francis preaching to the birds, St Giles' rescuing of the deer, or St Columba's saving of the crane that we simply overlook their theological significance. Many of the stories may appear sentimental, but none of them in fact are simply concerned with sentiment. Their purpose is deeply serious, and it is perhaps a sign of our lost innocence that we fail to see their cardinal relevance today. The key to understanding the example of the saints is surely found in this telling line from St Bonaventure. Speaking of St Francis he writes: 'When he considered the primordial source of all things, he was filled with even more abundant piety, calling creatures, no matter how small, by the name of brother or sister, because he knew that they had the same source as himself.' It is precisely because all living creatures have the same common Father that we can embrace each and every one as 'brother' and 'sister'. If Christ is the Logos through whom all things come to be, and if this Logos, as St Athanasius explains, permeates the universe 'illuminating all things visible and invisible, containing and enclosing them in himself', then it must follow that we are related christologically to all living things. Nothing in creation can therefore be really alien to us, and however fallen creation may be it still reflects the glory of God. In this way the saints continue and develop the deeply christological view of creation found in the New Testament. For what God does in Christ is not to be seen as an isolated act of love for humankind; rather, all creation is involved in the acts of incarnation and resurrection. 'And thus in this lifting up of the Incarnation of His Son, and in the glory of his resurrection according to the flesh,' writes St John of the Cross, 'not only did the Father beautify the creatures in part, but we can say that He left them all clothed with beauty and dignity.'

The love of the saints for animals is not, then, some sentimental gloss which may obscure their real teachings. On the contrary, the example of the saints is in many cases their teaching to us. It is precisely because of their closeness to God that they were able to feel a loving reverence for his creatures. 'Hast thou never learned in Holy Writ that he who led his life after God's will, the wild beasts and the wild birds have become more intimate with him?' asks St Guthlac. Or, as St Catherine of Siena puts it: 'The reason why God's servants love His creatures so deeply is that they realize how deeply Christ loves them.' 'And', she continues, 'this is the very character of love to love what is loved by those we love.'

In the articulation of this vision the theologian has a special role. 'It is good to realize', writes that great sage Francis Hugh Maycock, contemplating the beauty of nature, 'that God has other interests besides men!'[3] For it is vital to remember that the God of Abraham, Isaac, Jacob and Jesus Christ is not simply the God of human beings. 'It must never be forgotten', writes Austin Farrer, 'that God is the God of hawks no less than of sparrows, of microbes no less than of men.' Animals, in particular, have what E. F. Schumacher calls a 'meta-economic' value. They are not simply commodities or resources for human beings, but alive, sensitive beings endowed by God's Spirit. Because of this, cruelty must be anathematized. 'Think of your feelings at cruelty practised upon brute animals', says Cardinal Newman, 'and you will gain the sort of feeling which the history of Christ's Cross and Passion ought to excite within you.' Cruelty cannot co-exist with Christian love. 'Cruelty is Atheism', writes Humphry Primatt, that great seventeenth-century divine. 'Cruelty', he argues, is 'Infidelity' and 'the worst of Heresies'. How can it be otherwise if we believe in a loving, generous God?

It must be the task of the theologian to call us back to some of those basics without which we can lose that proper sense of ourselves as creatures in God's world. The AuSable Institute in Michigan, USA, dedicated to a systematic theological study of creation, has as its philosophy the following statement: 'God is the owner of all. Humankind is not the owner of that over which he has authority. Human authority is more that of trustee than owner. The scope of this trust is global. Since all creatures depend on the earth for life, health and fulfilment, stewardship is the responsible use and care of creation. This is the clear and repeated testimony of scripture'.[4] When we think of ourselves as owning or possessing creation for our own ends, we lapse into error. If we are to regain that sense of our moral dominion over animals, and avoid what W. H. Vanstone calls the 'anthropocentric theology of the last fifteen or twenty years' which is 'degenerating towards triviality',[5] then we must have a renewed vision of ourselves as global peacemakers.

But if we are to be renewed in vision, then we need the inspiration of poets as much as the example of saints and the teaching of sensitive theologians. For poets often have that intuitive grasp of the unity of creation and the universal claim of compassion. 'He bears in his heart all wounds', writes Edith Sitwell of the suffering Christ, who still suffers in our world because of the 'wounds of the baited bear . . . whom the keepers beat on his helpless flesh . . . the tears of the hunted hare'. For 'other eyes than ours', writes Christina Rossetti, 'were made to look on flowers', and each good creature has 'just as good a right to its appointed portion of delight as any King'. Poets are one with the saints in bringing hope to our world, of stressing the need to hope in order to be fully human. As Tennyson wrote:

Oh yet we trust that somehow good,
will be the final goal of ill,
To pangs of nature, sins of will,
Defects of doubt, and taints of blood;

That nothing walks with aimless feet;
That not one life shall be destroy'd,
Or cast as rubbish to the void,
When God hath made the pile complete.

Few people have grasped the spiritual significance of Christ's experience in the wilderness more acutely, or offered more penetrating exegesis of Mark 1.12, than Robert Graves in his poem depicting Christ's solidarity with the 'poor, blind broken things, foul in their miseries'.

And ever with Him went,
Of all His wanderings
Comrade, with ragged coat,
Gaunt ribs – poor innocent –
Bleeding foot, burning throat,
The guileless old scapegoat;
For forty nights and days
Followed in Jesus' ways,
Sure guard behind Him kept,
Tears like a lover wept.

In the light of all this united testimony it is not surprising that the Churches this century have spoken and resolved at length, almost to the point of repetition, about the need to care for animals and to eschew cruelty. It was after all an Anglican clergyman, Arthur Broome, who called the first meeting in 1824 which led to the founding of the then SPCA, the first animal protection society in the world. He was the Society's first secretary, resigning his London living to work full-time for the cause, employing inspectors out of his own pocket and ending up in prison trying to pay for the debts of the Society. The first 'Prospectus' of the Society, published in June 1824, makes clear that the motivating force was nothing less than the 'great moral and Christian obligation of kindness and compassion towards the brute creation'.[6] The first Board of Managers included many notable Christians, in particular: William Wilberforce, Richard Martin, Dr Heslop, the Rector of Marylebone, and the Earl of Crawford. The new Society dedicated itself, among other things, to the 'establishment of periodical discourses, from the pulpit, in one or more metropolitan churches'.[7] A declaration in the first minute book maintained that the proceedings of the Society were 'entirely based on the Christian Faith, and on Christian Principles'.[8]

For the centenary of the Society, the poet Thomas Hardy wrote 'An Ode' entitled 'Compassion' to celebrate the advance of the pioneering work:

Much has been won – more, maybe, than we know
And on we labour hopeful. 'Ailinon!'
A mighty voice calls: 'But may the good prevail!'
And 'Blessed are the merciful!'
Calls a yet mightier one.

In 1977 the then Archbishop of Canterbury, Dr Donald Coggan, on accepting the presidency of the Society issued this unequivocal statement: 'I am happy to follow the lead given to the Church some 150 years ago by the London vicar who called the meeting in 1824 which led to the Society's foundation.' 'There have always been', he continued, 'and still are many Churchmen, both lay and ordained, who have seen it as part of their Christian profession to work for animal welfare. I want to offer my support to the RSPCA because without their constant vigilance and the devoted work of their Officers and Inspectors the level of unnecessary animal suffering in this country would be so much higher.' 'Animals, as part of God's creation,' he insisted, 'have rights which must be respected. It behoves us always to be sensitive to their needs and to the reality of their pain.'

Yet Christian compassion, if it is to be sustained and constant and real, needs the support and inspiration of Christian liturgy and worship. It was Laurens van der Post who insisted that we 'must turn back to what we have left of the capacity for wonder'. 'Only reverence for life', he wrote, 'can deliver us from our inhumanity, and from the cataclysm of violence awaiting us at the end of our present road.'[9] By focusing our minds on God the Creator, and reminding us that we are all fellow creatures in his world, worship can invigorate and refresh our humanity. The Spirit of Christ can make all things new – even and especially the frequently dull sensitivities of modern men and women. 'In his way to union with God', writes Vladimir Lossky, that great exponent of the Eastern tradition, 'man in no way leaves creatures aside, but gathers together in his love the whole cosmos disordered by sin, that it may at last be transfigured by grace.' If we are to become loving people then we must celebrate God the Creator and praise him. For in so doing, Scripture reminds us, we do no less than the humblest of creation, 'beasts and all cattle, creeping things and flying birds' all praise the Lord (see Psalm 148.7–10).

For this reason alone we should welcome the increasing number of prayers, litanies, meditations and benedictions concerned to celebrate our being-with-creation, and especially those which focus the need for healing of the animal creation. Humans, alone in creation, have a terrible capacity to make good or ill, to injure thoughtlessly or to live in peace. We need spiritual resources to fulfil what Edward Carpenter calls the 'divine task of lifting up creation, redeeming those orders of which [we form] a part, and directing them towards their end.' By the power of God's Spirit, we co-operate with the pattern of redemption by allowing ourselves to become redeemers.

According to the Christian reckoning of things, we ourselves are inextricably caught up with the plight of unredeemed creation. The misery of animals, their fate and suffering, is a sign to us of what life without compassion can produce, as much for fellow humans as for fellow creatures. There is an indivisibility, a unity in all life which we threaten by needless harm, and that harm adversely affects us all. 'There are times', argues John Austin Baker, Bishop of Salisbury, 'when we have to take the lives of the more developed sentient creatures, either in mercy or in self-defence.' 'But how sad it is', he continues, 'when . . . we violate a genuine awareness, yes, we must say of the holiness of life, by needless killing.' 'Yet saddest of all, most terrible of all fates surely,' warns the Bishop, 'is to have lost that sense of the holiness of life altogether, to be so unaware of the true nature of the creatures with which we are dealing that we commit the blasphemy, the sacrilege, of bringing thousands of lives to a cruel and terrifying death, or of making those lives a living death – *and feel nothing*.'

It may well be that Schweitzer was right, and that not until we extend the circle of compassion to include

C. F. A.—2

all living things shall we ourselves know peace. We hope that this collection will help Christians to remember and recollect their tradition and, in so doing, become agents of the gospel for which all creatures long.

NOTES

1. Robin Attfield, *The Ethics of Environmental Concern* (Oxford, Basil Blackwell, 1983), p. 29.
2. Robert M. Grant and David N. Freeman, *The Secret Sayings of Jesus According to the Gospel of Thomas* (London, Fontana, 1960), p. 115.
3. Francis Hugh Maycock, 'Borneo Diary' in A. M. Allchin *et al.*, *Francis Hugh Maycock: A Tribute* (Oxford, SLG Press, 1981).
4. Philosophy of the AuSable Institute, cited and discussed in Wesley Granberg-Michaelson (ed.), *Tending the Garden: Essays on the Gospel and the Earth* (Grand Rapids, Michigan, Erdmans, 1987), p. vii.
5. W. H. Vanstone, 'On the Being of Nature' in *Theology* (July 1977).
6. 'Prospectus of the SPCA', in *RSPCA Records*, vol. II (1823–6), p. 201. We are grateful to the Librarian of the RSPCA for help in finding this document.
7. ibid., p. 202.
8. RSPCA Minute Book, No. 1, pp. 38–41, cited and discussed in James Turner, *Reckoning with the Beast: Animals, Pain and Humanity in the Victorian Mind* (New Jersey, The Johns Hopkins University Press, 1980), p. 43.
9. Laurens van der Post, cited on Poster 12 (London, USPG, 1985).
References to all other quotations are given in the text of the book. All biblical references are from the Revised Standard Version (RSV).

I

Creation

Readings

===

In the beginning God created the heavens and the earth . . . And God said, 'Let the waters bring forth swarms of living creatures, and let birds fly above the earth across the firmament of the heavens.' So God created the great sea monsters and every living creature that moves, with which the waters swarm, according to their kinds, and every winged bird according to its kind. And God saw that it was good. And God blessed them saying, 'Be fruitful and multiply and fill the waters in the seas, and let birds multiply on the earth.' And there was evening and there was morning, a fifth day.

And God said, 'Let the earth bring forth living creatures according to their kinds: cattle and creeping things and beasts of the earth according to their kinds.' And it was so. And God made the beasts of the earth according to their kinds and the cattle according to their kinds, and everything that creeps upon the ground according to its kind. And God saw that it was good.

Genesis 1.1, 20–5

Bless the Lord, O my soul!
O Lord my God, thou art very great . . .
Thou makest springs gush forth in the valleys;
    they flow between the hills,
they give drink to every beast of the field;
    the wild asses quench their thirst.

By them the birds of the air have their habitation;
   they sing among the branches.
From thy lofty abode thou waterest the mountains;
   the earth is satisfied with the fire of thy work.

Thou dost cause the grass to grow for the cattle,
   and plants for man to cultivate;
that he may bring forth food from the earth,
   and wine to gladden the heart of man,
oil to make his face shine,
   and bread to strengthen man's heart.
The trees of the Lord are watered abundantly,
   the cedars of Lebanon which he planted.
In them the birds build their nests;
   the stork has her home in the fir trees.
The high mountains are for the wild goats;
   the rocks are a refuge for the badgers.
Thou hast made the moon to mark the seasons;
   the sun knows its time for setting.
Thou makest darkness, and it is night,
   when all the beasts of the forest creep forth.
The young lions roar for their prey,
   seeking their food from God.
When the sun rises, they get them away
   and lie down in their dens.
Man goes forth to his work
   and to his labour until the evening.
O Lord, how manifold are thy works!
   In wisdom hast thou made them all;
   the earth is full of thy creatures.
Yonder is the sea, great and wide,
   which teems with things innumerable,
   living things both small and great.
There go the ships,
   and Leviathan which thou didst form
     to sport in it.

These all look to thee,
  to give them their food in due season.
When thou givest to them, they gather it up;
  when thou openest thy hand,
    they are filled with good things.
When thou hidest thy face, they are dismayed;
  when thou takest away their breath,
  they die and return to their dust.
When thou sendest forth thy Spirit,
    they are created;
  and thou renewest the face of the ground.

Psalm 104.1, 10–30

Praise the Lord from the earth,
  you sea monsters and all deeps,
fire and hail, snow and frost,
  stormy wind fulfilling his command!

Mountains and all hills,
  fruit trees and all cedars!
Beasts and all cattle,
  creeping things and flying birds!

Psalm 148.7–10

Hear, O my people, and I will speak,
   O Israel, I will testify against you.
   I am God, your God.
I do not reprove you for your sacrifices;
   your burnt offerings are continually before me.
I will accept no bull from your house,
   nor he-goat from your folds.
For every beast of the forest is mine,
   the cattle on a thousand hills.
I know all the birds of the air,
   and all that moves in the field is mine.

Psalm 50.7–11

For thou lovest all things that exist, and hast loathing for none of the things which thou hast made, for thou wouldst not have made anything if thou hadst hated it. How would anything have endured if thou hadst not willed it? Or how would anything not called forth by thee have been preserved? Thou sparest all things, for they are thine, O Lord who lovest the living. For thy immortal spirit is in all things.

Wisdom of Solomon 11.24—12.1

Look at the birds of the air; they neither sow nor reap nor gather into barns, and yet your heavenly Father feeds them.

Matthew 6.26

Are not five sparrows sold for two pennies? And not one of them is forgotten before God.

Luke 12.6

And round the throne, on each side of the throne, are four living creatures, full of eyes in front and behind: the first living creature like a lion, the second living creature like an ox, the third living creature with the face of a man, and the fourth living creature like a flying eagle. And the four living creatures, each of them with six wings, are full of eyes all round and within, and day and night they never cease to sing,

'Holy, holy, holy, is the Lord God Almighty,
who was and is and is to come!'

And whenever the living creatures give glory and honour and thanks to him who is seated on the throne, who lives for ever and ever, the twenty-four elders fall down before him who is seated on the throne and worship him who lives for ever and ever; they cast their crowns before the throne, singing,

'Worthy art thou, our Lord and God,
to receive glory and honour and power,
for thou didst create all things,
and by thy will they existed and were created.'

Revelation 4.6b–11

Cattle and wild beasts pray, and bend their knees, and in coming forth from their stalls and lairs look up to heaven, their mouths not idle, making the spirit move in their fashion. Moreover the birds taking flight lift themselves up to heaven and, instead of hands, spread out the cross of their wings, while saying something which may be supposed to be a prayer.

Tertullian

[The Logos] produces a single melody . . . holding the universe like a lyre, draws together the things in the air with those on earth, and those in the heaven with those in the air, and combines the whole with the parts, linking them with his command and will, and thus producing in beauty and harmony a single world and a single order within it . . . [The Logos] extends his power everywhere, illuminating all things visible and invisible, containing and enclosing them in himself, [giving] life and everything, everywhere, to each individually and to all together creating an exquisite single euphonious harmony.

St Athanasius

For when he considers the universe, can anyone be so simple-minded as not to believe that the Divine is present in everything, pervading, embracing and penetrating it? For all things depend upon Him who is, and nothing can exist which does not have its being in Him who is.

St Gregory of Nyssa

It would be ridiculous . . . to regard the defects of beasts, trees and other mutable and mortal things . . . as deserving of condemnation. Such defects do indeed effect the decay of their nature, which is liable to dissolution; but these creatures have received their mode of being by the will of their Creator, whose purpose is that they should bring to perfection the beauty of the lower parts of the universe by their alteration and succession in the passage of the seasons; and this is a beauty in its own kind, finding its place among the constituent parts of the world . . . Therefore it is the nature of things considered in itself, without regard to our convenience or inconvenience, that gives glory to the Creator . . . And so all nature's substances are good, because they exist and therefore have their own mode and kind of being, and, in their fashion, a peace and harmony among themselves.

St Augustine of Hippo

The creatures of the sense world signify the invisible attributes of God, partly because God is the origin, exemplar and end of every creature, and every effect is the sign of its cause, the exemplification of its exemplar and the path to the end, to which it leads . . . For every creature is by its nature a kind of effigy and likeness of the eternal Wisdom.

Therefore, open your eyes, alert the ears of your spirit, open your lips and apply your heart so that in all creatures you may see, hear, praise, love and worship, glorify and honour your God.

St Bonaventure

And in this he showed me something small, no bigger than a hazel-nut, lying in the palm of my hand, and I perceived that it was as round as any ball. I looked at this and thought: What can this be? And I was given this general answer: It is everything which is made. I was amazed that it could last, for I thought that it was so little that it could suddenly fall into nothing. And I was answered in my understanding: It lasts and always will, because God loves it; and thus everything has being through the love of God. In this little thing I saw three properties. The first is that God made it, the second is that he loves it, the third is that God pre-serves it. But what is that to me? It is that God is the Creator and the lover and the protector.

Julian of Norwich

And if thy heart be straight with God, then every creature shall be to thee a mirror of life and a book of holy doctrine, for there is no creature so little or so vile, but that sheweth and representeth the goodness of God.

Thomas à Kempis

And I have felt
A presence that disturbs me with the joy
Of elevated thoughts . . .
A motion and a spirit, that impels
All thinking things, all objects of all thought,
And rolls through all things. Therefore am I still
A lover of the meadows and the woods,
And mountains; and of all that we behold
From this green earth . . .

William Wordsworth

All nature owns with one accord
The great and universal Lord:
Insect and bird and tree and flower –
The witnesses of every hour –
Are pregnant with his prophecy
And, 'God be with us', all reply.
The first link in the mighty plan
Is still – and all unbraideth man.

John Clare

Yes, God is good – in earth and sky,
From ocean depths and spreading wood,
Ten thousand voices seem to cry:
God made us all, and God is good.

The merry birds prolong the strain,
Their song with every spring renewed;
And balmy air, and falling rain,
Each softly whispers: God is good.

John Hampden Gurney

Ever fresh the broad creation,
A divine improvisation,
From the heart of God proceeds,
A single will, a million deeds . . .

He is the heart of every creature;
He is the meaning of each feature;
And his mind is in the sky,
Than all it holds more deep, more high.

Ralph Waldo Emerson

If you have heard the singing of the birds or the running of the stream, or the voices of children as you came to church, then reflect it was Christ who caused you to hear them. He fills the earth and the air with all melodies, and He gives to men the power of taking them in.

F. D. Maurice

Love all God's creation, the whole of it and every grain of sand. Love every leaf, every ray of God's light! Love the animals, love the plants, love everything. If you love everything, you will perceive the divine mystery in things. And once you have perceived it, you will begin to comprehend it ceaselessly, more and more every day. And you will at last come to love the whole world with an abiding, universal love. Love the animals: God has given them the rudiments of thought and untroubled joy. Do not, therefore, trouble it, do not torture them, do not deprive them of their joy, do not go against God's intent.

Fyodor Mikhail Dostoevsky

It must never be forgotten that God is the God of hawks no less than of sparrows, of microbes no less than of men.

Austin Farrer

And other eyes than ours
Were made to look on flowers,
Eyes of small birds and insects small:
The deep sun-blushing rose
Round which the prickles close
Opens her bosom to them all.
The tiniest living thing
That soars on feathered wing,
Or crawls among the long grass out of sight
Has just as good a right
To its appointed portion of delight
As any King.

Christina Rossetti

And for all this, nature is never spent;
There lives the dearest freshness deep down
things . . .
Because the Holy Ghost over the bent
World broods with warm breast and with ah! bright
wings.

Gerard Manley Hopkins

Prayers

You alone are unutterable,
from the time you created all things
    that can be spoken of.
You alone are unknowable,
from the time you created all things
    that can be known.
All things cry out about you;
those which speak,
    and those which cannot speak.
All things honour you;
those which think,
    and those which cannot think.
For there is one longing, one groaning,
    that all things have for you . . .

All things pray to you that comprehend
    your plan
and offer you a silent hymn.
In you, the One, all things abide,
and all things endlessly run to you
who are the end of all.

St Gregory Nazianzen

Most High, Omnipotent, Good Lord.
Thine be the praise, the glory, the honour, and all
*   benediction.*
To Thee alone, Most High, they are due,
and no man is worthy to mention Thee.

Be Thou praised, my Lord, with all Thy creatures,
above all Brother Sun,
who gives the day and lightens us therewith.

And he is beautiful and radiant with great splendour,
of Thee, Most High, he bears similitude.

Be Thou praised, my Lord, of Sister Moon and the stars,
in the heaven has Thou formed them, clear and precious
*   and comely.*

Be Thou praised, my Lord, of Brother Wind,
and of the air and the cloud, and of fair and of all weather,
by the which Thou givest to Thy creatures sustenance.

Be Thou praised, my Lord, of Sister Water,
which is much useful and humble and precious and pure.

Be Thou praised, my Lord, of Brother Fire,
by which Thou has lightened the night,
and he is beautiful and joyful and robust and strong.

Be Thou praised, my Lord, of our Sister Mother Earth,
which sustains and hath us in rule,
and produces divers fruits with coloured flowers and herbs.

Be Thou praised, my Lord, of those who pardon for Thy
*   love*
and endure sickness and tribulations.

Blessed are they who will endure it in peace,
for by Thee, Most High, they shall be crowned.

Be Thou praised, my Lord, of our Sister Bodily Death,
from whom no man living may escape.
Woe to those who die in mortal sin:

Blessed are they who are found in Thy most holy will,
for the second death shall not work them ill.

Praise ye and bless my Lord, and give Him thanks,
and serve Him with great humility.

St Francis of Assisi

O all ye Works of the Lord, bless ye the Lord:
praise him, and magnify him for ever . . .
O let the Earth bless the Lord:
yea, let it praise him, and magnify him for ever . . .
O all ye Green Things upon the Earth, bless ye the Lord:
praise him, and magnify him for ever.
O ye Wells, bless ye the Lord:
praise him, and magnify him for ever.
O ye Seas and Floods, bless ye the Lord:
praise him, and magnify him for ever.
O ye Whales, and all that move in the Waters,
    bless ye the Lord:
praise him, and magnify him for ever.
O all ye Fowls of the Air, bless ye the Lord:
praise him, and magnify him for ever.
O all ye Beasts and Cattle, bless ye the Lord:
praise him, and magnify him for ever.

The Book of Common Prayer

I sing the goodness of the Lord
That filled the earth with food;
He formed the creatures with His word,
And then pronounced them good.

Creatures, as numerous as they be,
Are subject to Thy care;
There's not a place where we can flee
But God is present there.

Isaac Watts

All creatures of our God and King,
Lift up your voice and with us sing
   Alleluia, alleluia!
Thou burning sun with golden beam,
Thou silver moon with softer gleam . . .

Dear mother earth, who day by day
Unfoldest blessings on our way,
   O praise Him, alleluia!
The flowers and fruits that in thee grow,
Let them His glory also show . . .

Let all things their Creator bless,
And worship Him in humbleness.
   O praise Him, alleluia!
Praise, praise the Father, praise the Son,
And praise the Spirit, Three in One:

   O praise Him, O praise Him,
   Alleluia, alleluia, alleluia!

William Henry Draper

O Thou, Who givest to the woodland wren
A throat, like to the little light-set door,
That opens to his early joy – to men
The spirit of true worship, which is more
Than all this sylvan rapture: what a world
Is Thine, O Lord! – skies, earth, men, beasts and birds!
The poet and the painter have unfurl'd
Their love and wonder in descriptive words,
Or sprightly hues – each, after his own sort,
Emptying his heart of its delicious hoards;
But all self-conscious blazonry comes short
Of that still sense no active mood affords,
Ere yet the brush is dipt, or utter'd phrase
Hath breathed abroad those folds of silent praise!

Charles Tennyson Turner

My soul, praise, praise the Lord!
O God, thou art great:
In fathomless works
Thyself Thou dost hide.
Before Thy dark wisdom
And power uncreate,
Man's mind, that dare praise Thee,
In fear must abide.

All beasts of the field
Rejoice in their life;
Among the tall trees
Are light birds on wing;
With strains of their music
The woodlands are rife;
They nest in thick branches
And welcome sweet spring.

Robert Seymour Bridges

We praise Thee, O God, for Thy glory displayed in all the
creatures of the earth . . .

For all things exist only as seen by Thee, only as known
by Thee . . .

They affirm Thee in living: all things affirm Thee in
living; the bird in the air, both the hawk and the finch; the
beast on the earth, both the wolf and the lamb; the worm in
the soil and the worm in the belly.

T. S. Eliot

Let us praise our Maker, with true passion extol Him.
Let the whole creation give out another sweetness,
Nicer in our nostrils, a novel fragrance
From cleansed occasions in accord together
As one feeling fabric, all flushed and intact,
Phenomena and numbers announcing in one
Multitudinous oecumenical song
Their grand givenness of gratitude and joy,
Peaceable and plural, their positive truth
An authoritative This, an unthreatened Now
When, in love and in laughter, each lives itself,
For, united by His Word, cognition, power,
System and Order, are a single glory,
And the pattern is complex, their places safe.

W. H. Auden

O God I thank thee
for all the creatures thou hast made,
so perfect in their kind –
great animals like the elephant and the rhinoceros,
humorous animals like the camel and the monkey,
friendly ones like the dog and the cat,
working ones like the horse and the ox,
timid ones like the squirrel and the rabbit,
majestic ones like the lion and the tiger,
for birds with their songs.
O Lord give us such love for thy creation,
that love may cast out fear
and all thy creatures see in man
their priest and friend,
through Jesus Christ our Lord.

George Appleton

Most high, almighty and good Lord, grant your people grace to renounce gladly the vanities of this world; that, after the example of blessed Francis, we may for love of you delight in all your creatures, with perfectness of joy; through Jesus Christ our Lord, who lives and reigns with you and the Holy Spirit, One God, now and for ever.

We give you thanks most gracious God, for the beauty of the earth and sky and sea; for the richness of mountains, plains and rivers; for the songs of birds and the loveliness of flowers, and for the wonder of your animal kingdom. We praise you for these good gifts, and pray that we may safeguard them for our posterity. Grant that we may continue to grow in our grateful enjoyment of your abundant creation, to the honour and glory of your Name, now and for ever.

From the Earth Mass

2

Communion

Readings

==

In the day that the Lord God made the earth and the heavens, when no plant of the field was yet in the earth and no herb of the field had yet sprung up – for the Lord God had not caused it to rain upon the earth, and there was no man to till the ground; but a mist went up from the earth and watered the whole face of the ground – then the Lord God formed man of dust from the ground, and breathed into his nostrils the breath of life; and man became a living being . . .

Then the Lord God said, 'It is not good that the man should be alone; I will make him a helper fit for him.' So out of the ground the Lord God formed every beast of the field and every bird of the air, and brought them to the man to see what he would call them; and whatever the man called every living creature, that was its name.

Genesis 2.4b–7, 18–19

When men began to multiply on the face of the ground . . . God saw the earth, and behold, it was corrupt; for all flesh had corrupted their way upon the earth. And God said to Noah, 'I have determined to make an end of all flesh . . . behold, I will bring a flood of waters upon the earth, to destroy all flesh in which is the breath of life from under heaven; everything that is on the earth shall die. But I will establish my covenant with you; and you shall come into the ark, you, your sons, your wife, and your sons' wives with you. And of every living thing of all flesh, you shall bring two of every sort into the ark, to keep them alive with you; they shall be male and female . . .'

Of clean animals, and of animals that are not clean, and of birds, and of everything that creeps on the ground, two and two, male and female, went into the ark with Noah, as God had commanded Noah. And after seven days the waters of the flood came upon the earth . . . And all flesh died that moved upon the earth, birds, cattle, beasts, all swarming creatures that swarm upon the earth, and every man; everything on the dry land in whose nostrils was the breath of life died . . .

But God remembered Noah and all the beasts and all the cattle that were with him in the ark. And God made a wind blow over the earth, and the waters subsided; the fountains of the deep and the windows of the heavens were closed, the rain from the heavens was restrained . . .

Then God said to Noah, 'Go forth from the ark, you and your wife, and your sons and your sons' wives with you. Bring forth with you every living thing that is with you of all flesh – birds and animals and every creeping thing that creeps on the earth – that they may breed abundantly on the earth, and be fruitful and multiply upon the earth.'

. . . And God said, 'This is the sign of the covenant which I make between me and you and every living creature that is with you, for all future generations: I set my bow in the cloud, and it shall be a sign of the covenant between me and the earth. When I bring clouds over the earth and the bow is seen in the clouds, I will remember my covenant which is between me and you and every living creature of all flesh; and the waters shall never again become a flood to destroy all flesh.'

Genesis 6–9

For the fate of the sons of men and the fate of beasts is the same; as one dies, so dies the other. They all have the same breath, and man has no advantage over the beasts; for all is vanity. All go to one place; all are from the dust, and all turn to dust again. Who knows whether the spirit of man goes upward and the spirit of the beast goes down to the earth?

Ecclesiastes 3.19–21

The Spirit immediately drove him out into the wilderness. And he was in the wilderness forty days, tempted by Satan; and he was with the wild beasts; and the angels ministered to him.

Mark 1.12–13

Jesus sent two disciples, saying to them, 'Go into the village opposite you, and immediately you will find an ass tied, and a colt with her; untie them and bring them to me. If any one says anything to you, you shall say, "the Lord has need of them," and he will send them immediately.' This took place to fulfil what was spoken by the prophet, saying:
   'Tell the daughter of Zion,
   Behold, your king is coming to you,
   humble, and mounted on an ass,
   and on a colt, the foal of an ass.'

Matthew 21.1b–5

Hast thou never learned in Holy Writ that he who led his life after God's will, the wild beasts and the wild birds have become more intimate with him?

St Guthlac of Crowland

Shy creatures, such as stags, horses and birds were not afraid of him, nor did he fear wolves and snakes. All wild animals were his friends, disporting themselves in his company and fleeing to him in danger.

St Godric of Finchale

My little sisters the birds, much are ye beholden to God your Creator, and always and in every place ye ought to praise Him for that He hath given you a double and a triple vesture; He hath given you freedom to go into every place, and also did preserve the seed of you in the ark of Noe, in order that your kind might not perish from the earth. Again, ye are beholden to Him for the element of the air which he hath appointed for you; moreover ye sow not, neither do ye reap, and God feedeth you and giveth you the rivers and the fountains for your drink . . . wherefore your Creator loveth you much, since He hath dealt so bounteously with you; and therefore beware, little sisters mine, of the sin of ingratitude, but ever strive to praise God.

St Francis of Assisi

O thou Little Brother, that brimmest with full heart, and having naught, possessest all, surely thou dost well to sing! For thou hast life without labour and beauty without burden, and riches without care. When thou wakest, lo, it is dawn; and when thou comest to sleep it is eve. And when thy two wings lie folded about thy heart, lo, there is rest. Therefore sing, Brother, having this great wealth, that when thou singest thou givest thy riches to all.

St Francis of Assisi

Ye fishes, my brothers, much are ye bound, according to your power, to thank God our Creator, who hath given you so noble an element for your habitation . . . God, your Creator, bountiful and kind, when He created you, commanded you to increase and multiply, and gave you His blessing; then in the universal deluge and when all other animals were perishing, you alone did God preserve from harm. Moreover, He hath given you fins that ye may fare whithersoever it may please you. To you it was granted, by commandment of God, to preserve Jonah the prophet, and after the third day to cast him forth on dry land safe and whole. Ye did offer the tribute money to Christ our Lord, to Him poor little one, that had not wherewithal to pay. Ye, by a mystery, were the food of the eternal King, Christ Jesus, before the resurrection and after. For all those things much are ye held to praise and bless God, that hath given you blessings so manifold and so great; yea, even more than to any other of his creatures.

St Anthony of Padua

The reason why God's servants love His creatures so deeply is that they realize how deeply Christ loves them. And this is the very character of love to love what is loved by those we love.

St Catherine of Siena

Here I saw a great unity between Christ and us, as I understand it; for when he was in pain we were in pain, and all creatures able to suffer pain suffered with him.

Julian of Norwich

He prayeth best, who loveth best
All things both great and small;
For the dear God who loveth us,
He made and loveth all.

Samuel Taylor Coleridge

God made all the creatures and gave
them our love and our fear,
To give sign, we and they are His
Children, one family here.

Robert Browning

I think I could turn and live with animals,
they are so placid and self-contain'd,
I stand and look at them long and long.

They do not sweat and whine about their condition,
They do not lie awake in the dark and weep for their
  sins,
They do not make me sick discussing their duty to
  God,
Not one is dissatisfied, not one is demented with the
  mania of owning things . . .
Not one is respectable or unhappy over the whole
  earth.

Walt Whitman

Without perfect sympathy with the animals around
them, no gentleman's education, no Christian education, could be of any possible use.

John Ruskin

In former days all animals could speak and so could
the flowers, the trees and the stones and all lifeless
things who were all created by the same God who had
created man. Therefore man should be kind to the
animals, and treat all lifeless things as if they could still
hear and understand. On the day of the Last Judgement the animals would be called in first by God to
give evidence against the dead man. Only after the
animals had had their say would his fellow creatures
be called in as witnesses.

Axel Munthe

Our ancestors sinned in ignorance; they were taught (as I deeply regret to say one great Christian Church still teaches) that the world, with all that it contains, was made for man, and that the lower orders of creation have no claims whatever upon us. But we no longer have the excuse of saying that we do not know; we do know that organic life on this planet is all woven of one stuff, and if we are children of our Heavenly Father, it must be true, as Christ told us, that no sparrow falls to the ground without his care. The new knowledge has revolutionized our ideas of our relations to the other living creatures who share the world with us, and it is our duty to consider seriously what this knowledge should mean for us in matters of conduct.

William Ralph Inge

I could not but feel with a sympathy full of regret all the pain that I saw around me, not only that of men, but that of the whole creation. From this community of suffering, I have never tried to withdraw myself. It seemed to me a matter of course that we should all take our share of the burden of suffering which lies upon the world.

Albert Schweitzer

Once the old Christian idea of a total difference in kind between man and beast has been abandoned, then no argument for experiments on animals can be found which is not also an argument for experiments on inferior men. If we cut up beasts simply because they cannot prevent us and because we are backing up our own side in the struggle for existence, it is only logical to cut up imbeciles, criminals, enemies or capitalists for the same reason.

C. S. Lewis

Existence can only become a home if the relationship between nature and human beings is without stresses and strains – if it can be described in terms of reconciliation, peace and a viable symbiosis. The indwelling of human beings in the natural system of the earth corresponds, for its part, to the indwelling of the Spirit in the soul and body of the human being, which puts an end to the alienation of human beings from themselves.

Jürgen Moltmann

Christ of His gentleness
Thirsting and hungering
Walked in the wilderness;
Soft words of grace He spoke
Unto lost desert-folk
That listened wondering.
He heard the bitterns call
From the ruined palace-wall,
Answered them brotherly;
He held communion

With the she-pelican
Of lonely piety.
Basilisk, cockatrice,
Flocked to His homilies,
With mail of dread device,
With monstrous barbed slings,
With eager dragon-eyes;
Great rats on leather wings,
And poor blind broken things,
Foul in their miseries.
And ever with Him went,
Of all His wanderings
Comrade, with ragged coat,
Gaunt ribs – poor innocent –
Bleeding foot, burning throat,
The guileless old scapegoat;
For forty nights and days
Followed in Jesus' ways,
Sure guard behind Him kept,
Tears like a lover wept.

Robert Graves

Believe me, birds, you need not fear,
No cages or limed twigs are here,
We only ask to live with you
In this green garden too . . .

And never will the thought of spring
Visit our minds, but a gold wing
Will flash among the green and blue,
And we'll remember you.

Sylvia Lynd

St Francis is before us also as an example of unalterable meekness and sincere love with regard to irrational beings who make up part of creation. In him re-echoes that harmony that is illustrated with striking words in the first pages of the Bible: 'God placed man in the garden of Eden to cultivate it and care for it' (Genesis 2.15), and he 'brought the animals to man to see what he would name them' (Genesis 2.19). In St Francis we glimpse almost an anticipation of that peace proposed by Sacred Scripture, when 'the wolf shall dwell with the lamb, and the leopard shall lie down with the kid, and the calf and the lion shall graze together, and a child shall lead them' (Isaiah 11.16). He looked upon creation with the eyes of one who could recognize in it the marvellous work of the hand of God. His voice, his glance, his solicitous care, not only towards men, but also towards animals and nature in general, are a faithful echo of the love with which God in the beginning pronounced his 'fiat' which had brought them into existence. How can we not feel vibrating in the Canticle of the Creatures something of the transcendent joy of God the Creator, of whom it is written that 'he saw everything that he had made, and behold it was very good' (Genesis 1.31)? Do we perhaps not have here an explanation for the sweet name of 'brother' and 'sister' with which the Poverello addressed every created being?

We too are called to a similar attitude. Created in the image of God, we must make him present among creatures 'as intelligent and noble masters and guardians of nature and not as heedless exploiters and destroyers' (Encyclical Letter, *Redemptor Hominis*, 15).

Pope John Paul II

Prayers

O God, enlarge within us the sense of
fellowship with all living things,
our brothers the animals to whom thou
gavest the earth as their home in
common with us.

We remember with shame that in the past
we have exercised the high dominion
of man with ruthless cruelty
so that the voice of the earth,
which should have gone up to thee
in song, has been a groan of travail.

May we realize that they live not for
us alone but for themselves and for
thee, and that they love the
sweetness of life.

St Basil the Great

To all the humble beasts there be,
To all the birds on land and sea,
Great Spirit sweet protection give,
That free and happy they may live!

And to our hearts the rapture bring
Of love for every living thing;
Make of us all one kin, and bless
Our ways with Christ's own gentleness.

John Galsworthy

Shatter, my God,
through the daring of your revelation
the childishly timid outlook
that can conceive of nothing greater
or more vital in the world
than the pitiable perfection
of our human organism.

Teilhard de Chardin

O Lord, how small is your creature, man!
Made in your image, where is his mercy,
his generosity, his pity and his love?
'He behaved like an animal' they say.
But they are wrong, Lord,
for animals know more than they are saying.
Where is their malice, their envy,
*   their corruption, their spite?*
Lord, give grace to your creature, man,
*   that he may be more like the animals.*
Amen.

Penelope Fleming

Lord,
I keep watch!
If I am not here
who will guard their house?
Watch over their sheep?
Be faithful?
No one but You and I
understands
what faithfulness is.
They call me, 'Good dog! Nice dog!'
Words . . .
I take their pats
and the old bones they throw me
and I seem pleased.
They really believe they make me happy.
I take kicks too
when they come my way.
None of that matters. I keep watch!
Lord, do not let me die
until, for them,
all danger is driven away.
Amen.

Carmen Bernos de Gasztold

We beseech thee, O Lord,
to hear our supplications on behalf
*   of the dumb creation,*
who after their kind bless, praise
*   and magnify thee.*
Grant that all cruelty to animals
*   may cease in our land;*
and deepen our thankfulness to thee
*   for the faithful companionship*
*   of those whom we delight to call*
*   our friends;*
for Jesus Christ's sake.

Source unknown

We pray for farm animals,
especially those living lives
distorted by suffering
in order to satisfy
human greed.
Grant that the human race
may realize
that animals are our fellow creatures,
and that God is concerned
about them, too;
through Jesus Christ our Lord.

J. R. Worsdall

O God,
you want the well-being of all creation.
Take all the violence away from us.
Curb the passion
that makes us destroy and exploit.
Give us peace on earth
by the power of Jesus Christ,
your Son here among us.
We ask and implore you
to grant us this,
for all humanity and for
our brothers and sisters in creation.

From the Creation Harvest Service

3

Responsibility

Readings

==

God said, 'Let us make man in our image, after our
likeness; and let them have dominion over the fish of
the sea, and over the birds of the air, and over the
cattle, and over all the earth, and over every creeping
thing that creeps upon the earth.' So God created man
in his own image, in the image of God he created him;
male and female he created them. And God blessed
them, and God said to them, 'Be fruitful and multiply,
and fill the earth and subdue it; and have dominion
over the fish of the sea and over the birds of the air
and over every living thing that moves upon the
earth.' And God said, 'Behold, I have given you every
plant yielding seed which is upon the face of all the
earth, and every tree with seed in its fruit; you shall
have them for food. And to every beast of the earth,
and to every bird of the air, and to everything that
creeps on the earth, everything that has the breath of
life, I have given every green plant for food.' And it
was so. And God saw everything that he had made,
and behold, it was very good.

Genesis 1.26–31

O Lord, our Lord,
how majestic is thy name in all the earth!

When I look at thy heavens, the work of thy fingers,
   the moon and the stars which thou hast
     established;
what is man that thou art mindful of him,
   and the son of man that thou dost care for him?

Yet thou hast made him little less than God,
    and dost crown him with glory and honour.
Thou hast given him dominion over the works of
    thy hands;
    thou hast put all things under his feet,
all sheep and oxen,
    and also the beasts of the field,
the birds of the air, and the fish of the sea,
    whatever passes along the paths of the sea.

O Lord, our Lord,
    how majestic is thy name in all the earth!

Psalm 8.1, 3–9

You shall not see your brother's ox or his sheep go
astray, and withhold your help from them; you shall
take them back to your brother. And if he is not near
you, or if you do not know him, you shall bring it
home to your house, and it shall be with you until
your brother seeks it; then you shall restore it to
him . . . You shall not see your brother's ass or his ox
fallen down by the way, and withhold your help from
them; you shall help him to lift them up again.

Deuteronomy 22.1–2, 4

And they asked him, 'Is it lawful to heal on the sabbath?' so that they might accuse him. He said to them,
'What man of you, if he has one sheep and it falls into
a pit on the sabbath, will not lay hold of it and lift it
out? Of how much more value is a man than a sheep!
So it is lawful to do good on the sabbath.'

Matthew 12.10b–12

I am the good shepherd. The good shepherd lays down his life for the sheep.

John 10.11

If I were to speak to the Emperor, I would, supplicating and persuading him tell him for the love of God and me to make a special law that no man should take or kill sister Larks, nor do them any harm. Likewise that all the Podestas of the towns, and the Lords of castles and villages, should be bound every year on Christmas day to compel men to throw wheat and other grains outside the cities and castles, that our sister Larks may have something to eat, and also the other birds, on a day of such solemnity. And that for the reverence of the Son of God, Who rested on that night with the Most Blessed Virgin Mary between an Ox and an Ass in the manger, whoever shall have an Ox and an Ass shall be bound to provide for them on that night the best of good fodder. Likewise on that day, all poor men should be satisfied by the rich with good food.

St Francis of Assisi

But it must be remembered that men are required to practise justice even in dealing with animals. Solomon condemns injustice to our neighbours the more severely when he says 'a just man cares well for his beasts' [Proverbs 12.10]. In a word, we are to do what is right voluntarily and freely, and each of us is responsible for doing his duty.

John Calvin

What wages doth the Lord desire of you for his earth that he giveth to you teachers, and great men, and to all the sons of men, and all creatures, but that you give him the praises, and the thanks, and the glory; and not that you should spend the creatures upon your lusts, but to do good with them; you that have much, to them that have little; and so to honour God with your substance; for nothing brought you into the world, nor nothing shall you take out of the world, but leave all creatures behind you as you found them . . .

George Fox

[On Psalm 36:] He [the Psalmist] observeth here that God by a comprehensive possession, and by way of eminence, enjoyeth the whole world; all mankind and all the Earth, with all that is therein, being His peculiar treasures. Since therefore we are made in the Image of God to live in His similitude, as they are His, they must be our treasures. We being wise and righteous over all as He is.

Thomas Traherne

I cannot think it extravagant to imagine, that mankind are no less, in proportion, accountable for the ill use of their dominion over creatures of the lower rank of beings, than for the exercise of tyranny over their own species.

Alexander Pope

[I] was early convinced in my mind that true religion consisted in an inward life, wherein the heart doth love and reverence God the Creator and learn to exercise true justice and goodness not only toward all men but also toward the brute creatures; that as the mind was moved on an inward principle to love God as an invisible, incomprehensible being, on the same principle it was moved to love him in all his manifestations in the visible world; and as by his breath the flame of life was kindled in all animal and sensitive creatures, to say we love God as unseen and at the same time exercise cruelty toward the least creature moving by his life, or by life derived from him was a contradiction in itself.

John Woolman

The seeds of cruelty, that since have swell'd
To such gigantic and enormous growth,
Were sown in human nature's fruitful soil.
Hence date the persecution and the pain
That man inflicts on all inferior kinds,
Regardless of their plaints.

William Cowper

To see a world in a grain of sand
And a heaven in a wild flower,
Hold infinity in the palm of your hand
And eternity in an hour.
A robin redbreast in a cage
Puts all Heaven in a rage.
A dove-house filled with doves and pigeons
Shudders Hell through all its regions.

A dog starved at his master's gate
Predicts the ruin of the state.
A horse misused upon the road
Calls to Heaven for human blood.
Each outcry of the hunted hare
A fibre from the brain does tear.
A skylark wounded in the wing,
A cherubim does cease to sing.
The gamecock clipped and armed for fight
Does the rising sun affright.
Every wolf's and lion's howl
Raises from Hell a human soul.
The wild deer wandering here and there
Keeps the human soul from care.
The lamb misused breeds public strife,
And yet forgives the butcher's knife.
The bat that flits at close of eve
Has left the brain that won't believe.
The owl that calls upon the night
Speaks the unbeliever's fright.
He who shall hurt the little wren
Shall never be beloved by men.
He who the ox to wrath has moved
Shall never be by woman loved.
The wanton boy that kills the fly
Shall feel the spider's enmity.
He who torments the chafer's sprite
Weaves a bower in endless night.
The caterpillar on the leaf
Repeats to thee thy mother's grief.
Kill not the moth nor butterfly,
For the Last Judgement draweth nigh.

William Blake

To delight in torture and pain of other creatures indifferently, natives or foreigners, of our own or of another species, kindred or no kindred, known or unknown; to feed as it were on death, and to be entertained with dying agonies; this has nothing in it accountable in the way of self-interest or private good . . . but is wholly and absolutely unnatural, as it is horrid and miserable.

Lord Shaftesbury

It is perfectly true that obligations and duties [exist] between moral persons, and that therefore the lower animals are not susceptible of those moral obligations which we owe to one another; but we owe a sevenfold obligation to the Creator of those animals. Our obligation and moral duty is to Him who made them, and, if we wish to know the limit and broad outline of our obligation, I say at once it is His nature, and His perfections, and among those perfections, one is most profoundly that of eternal mercy.

Cardinal Manning

Cruelty to animals is the degrading attitude of paganism.

Cardinal Hinsley

I am the voice of the voiceless;
Through me the dumb shall speak,
Till the deaf world's ear be made to hear
The wrongs of the wordless weak . . .

And I am my brother's keeper,
And I will fight his fight,
And speak the word for beast and bird,
Till the world shall set things right.

Ella Wheeler Wilcox

Riding through Ruwu swamp, about sunrise,
I saw the world awake; and as the ray
Touched the tall grasses where they sleeping lay,
Lo, the bright air alive with dragonflies:
With brittle wings aquiver, and great eyes
Piloting crimson bodies – slender and gay.
I aimed at one, and struck it, and it lay
Broken and lifeless, with fast fading dyes . . .
Then my soul sickened with a sudden pain
And horror at my own careless cruelty,
That in an idle moment I had slain
A creature whose sweet life it is to fly:
Like beasts that prey with tooth and claw . . .
Nay, they
Must slay to live, but what excuse had I?

Francis Brett Young

A flock of wild geese had settled to rest upon a pond. One of the flock had been captured by a gardener, who had clipped its wings before releasing it. When the geese started to resume their flight, this one tried frantically, but vainly, to lift itself into the air. The others, observing his struggles, flew about in obvious efforts to encourage him; but it was no use. Thereupon the entire flock settled back on the pond and waited, even though the urge to go on was strong within them. For several days they waited until the damaged feathers had grown sufficiently to permit the goose to fly. Meanwhile the unethical gardener, having been converted by the ethical geese, gladly watched them as they finally rose together, and all resumed their long flight.

Albert Schweitzer

A good hunter, honourable butcher and conscientious vivisectionist will differ from the bad in the fact that even as they are engaged in killing animals they hear this groaning and travailing of the creature, and therefore, in comparison with all others who have to do with animals, they are summoned to an intensified, sharpened and deepened diffidence, reserve and carefulness. In this matter they act on the extreme limits where respect for life and callous disregard jostle and may easily pass into one another. On these frontiers, if anywhere, animal protection, care and friendship are quite indispensable. Yet it is not only understandable but necessary that the affirmation of this whole possibility should always have been accompanied by a radical protest against it.

Karl Barth

Our society seems to be more and more orientated to over-production, to waste, and finally to production for destruction. Its orientation to global war is the culminating absurdity of its inner logic – or lack of logic. The mistreatment of animals in 'intensive husbandry' is, then, part of this larger picture of insensitivity to genuine values and indeed to humanity and life itself – a picture which more and more comes to display the ugly lineaments of what can only be called by its right name: barbarism.

Thomas Merton

The higher animals have an economic value because of their utility; but they have a meta-economic value in themselves. If I have a car, a man-made thing, I might legitimately argue that the best way to use it is never to bother about maintenance and simply run it to ruin. I may indeed have calculated that this is the most economical method of use. If the calculation is correct, nobody can criticize me for acting accordingly, for there is nothing sacred about a man-made thing like a car. But if I have an animal – be it only a calf or a hen – a living sensitive creature, am I allowed to treat it as nothing but a utility? Am I allowed to run it to ruin?

E. F. Schumacher

When I was young I often heard quoted a piece of Christian philosophy which was taken as self-evidently true. It was the proposition that animals have no rights. This, of course, is true only in one sense. They are not human persons and therefore they have no rights, so to speak, in their own right. But they have very positive rights because they are God's creatures. If we have to speak with absolute accuracy we must say that God has the right to have all his creatures treated with proper respect.

Nobody should therefore carelessly repeat the old saying that animals have no rights. This could easily lead to wanton cruelty. I speak of wanton cruelty because only the perverted are guilty of deliberate cruelty to animals or, indeed, to children. The difficulty is that many people do not realize the extent to which cruelty to animals is practised as a matter of business . . . It was once pointed out to me that the catechism had no question about cruelty to animals. This was true, but in giving lessons on Christian doctrine teachers now include the subject of cruelty to animals. The best and most experienced teachers do not, of course, talk of cruelty to animals. They talk of kindness to animals. Christians have a duty not only to refrain from doing harm but also to do positive good.

Cardinal Heenan

There have always been and still are many Churchmen, both lay and ordained, who have seen it as part of their Christian profession to work for animal welfare. I want to offer my support to the RSPCA because without their constant vigilance and the devoted work of their Officers and Inspectors the level of unnecessary animal suffering in this country would be so much higher. Animals, as part of God's creation, have rights which must be respected. It behoves us always to be sensitive to their needs and to the reality of their pain.

Donald Coggan

The soundest of all foundations on which to build a true and effective concern for animals is humility, reverence, awe in face of the mystery we call LIFE. There are times when we have to take the lives of the more developed sentient creatures, either in mercy or in self-defence. But how sad it is when, with no justification but that of material gain, we violate a genuine awareness, yes, we must say of the holiness of life, by needless killing . . . Yet saddest of all, most terrible of all fates surely, is to have lost that sense of the holiness of life altogether, to be so unaware of the true nature of the creatures with which we are dealing that we commit the blasphemy, the sacrilege of bringing thousands of lives to a cruel and terrifying death, or of making those lives a living death – *and feel nothing* . . . It is in the battery shed and the broiler house, not in the wild, that we find the true parallel to Auschwitz. Auschwitz is a purely human invention.

John Austin Baker

Prayers

====

For this I thank you,
That you have created me in your image,
And placed your wonders under my hands,
So that I may know them and rejoice in the works of your
   Creation.

I pray to you, eternal God,
Give me understanding and wisdom,
That I might not misuse your creation
But make use of it only for my needs
For the good of my neighbour, myself and my family.
Give me gratitude for all your gifts,
So that my mind does not say,
'This is mine, I have bought it.
I will possess it alone.
I am noble with it, majestic and beautiful;
It belongs to me because of this honour and glory.'
All this comes from the devil and the grievous fall of
   Adam.

Jacob Boehme

My Father, fill me with love for things beneath me.
Forbid that I should be cruel to the beast
  of the field.
Give me the tenderness that is born of reverence.
Teach me to revere the creation that is under me.
Was not its life a stream from Thy life?
Is not its life a mystery to me even now?
Does it not accomplish without reasoning
  what I cannot do by reasoning?
Let me uncover my head before the mystery.
Shall I bruise that which is so full of Thee,
  which surpasses me even while it obeys me?

George Matheson

Almighty God, who has ordained that man
  should have dominion over the beasts
 of the field and every living thing:
grant us the help of thy grace, that we
  may see in this a great responsibility;
give to all who deal with thy creatures
  a compassionate heart:
visit with thy justice those who are
  cruel to them, or hurt them needlessly;
and make us ever thankful for the joy
  of their companionship;
for the sake of him who, at the last,
  will gather all things to himself,
  and make all things new again,
  even Jesus Christ, our Lord.

Richard Tatlock

*Almighty God, we beseech Thee on behalf
    of the one hundred million animals
    which are sacrificed each year in the
    scientific laboratories of the world.
In Thy infinite compassion, gather
    these innocent and defenceless
    creatures into Thine arms and grant
    them Thy divine protection.
Soften the hearts of their captors,
    we pray, that the longing of all
    living things to be free might be
    fulfilled.
Open the ears of those who experiment
    upon animals that the painful cries
    of Thy creation might be heard.
Enlighten our minds that new ways for
    the gathering of information might
    be found.
We pray in the name of Him who blessed
    the merciful and promised them mercy,
    even Jesus Christ our Lord.*

Richard Newman

O God, source of life and power,
  Who feedeth the birds of the heavens,
increase our tenderness towards all the
  creatures of Thy hand.
Help us to refrain from petty acts of cruelty,
  or thoughtless deeds of harm to any
  living animal.
May we care for them at all times,
  especially during hard weather,
  and protect them from injury
  so that they learn to trust us as friends.
Let our sympathy grow with knowledge,
  so that the whole creation may rejoice
  in Thy presence.

Source unknown

Almighty God, Who hast created man
  in thine own image and hast set him
  in stewardship over Thy creatures
  of earth, sea, and sky;
grant us grace fearlessly to contend
  against evil, and to make no peace
  with oppression;
and, that we may reverently use our
  freedom, help us to employ it in
  the maintenance of justice among
  men and beasts,
to the glory of thy holy Name;
  through Jesus Christ our Lord.

Society of United Prayer for Animals

Almighty God,
you have given us
temporary lordship
of your beautiful creation.
But we have misused our power,
turned away from responsibility
and marred your image in us.
Forgive us, true Lord,
especially for our callousness
and cruelty to animals.
Help us to follow the way
of your Son, Jesus Christ,
who expressed power in humility
and lordship in loving service.

Enable us, by your Spirit,
to walk in newness of life,
healing injury, avoiding wrong
and making peace with all your creatures.

From the RSPCA Order of Service

Heavenly Father
your Holy Spirit
gives breath to all living things;
renew us by this same Spirit
that we may learn to respect
what you have given
and care for what you have made
through Jesus Christ
your Son, our Lord.

Almighty God
your Son, Jesus Christ,
taught us to love
even the least among us;
give us the courage to care
for all living creatures
and the strength to defend
even the weakest of all.

From the RSPCA Order of Service

O God, our Creator and Preserver,
we humbly confess our manifold sins
of ignorance and negligence,
and specially at this time,
towards thy creatures,
over whom thou hast given man
thy dominion.
We acknowledge with shame of heart
that we have oft-times
turned a deaf ear
to their piteous cry.
We have been content
to let custom have its way,
even when our hearts

have mourned its wickedness.
We most earnestly beseech thee
in the name of him thy Son
and our most blessed Lord,
who for our salvation
came down from heaven
and was cradled amongst the cattle,
to grant us true repentance
and thy gracious forgiveness,
through Jesus Christ our Lord.
Amen.

From the Animal Christian Concern Order of Service

We praise you for the creation of the world and all the living creatures in the earth, sky and sea.

We are thankful, O God.

For the gentle eyes of the deer, the friendship of dogs, the purr of cats, the strength of bears, the beauty of a hippo, the humour of chimps, the intelligence of gorillas, the grace of dolphins, and the magnificence of whales. Help us to keep them safe.

We are thankful, O God.

For the bond between all living creatures created by the same author, and for the memory of our kinship to the animal world kindled each time a rainbow appears.

We are thankful, O God.

Keep us mindful of the vision of the peaceable kingdom in which all living creatures dwell in harmony.

This we pray, O God.

Give us a voice to speak in protest when any of your beloved creatures are treated cruelly. Help us to be advocates for those innocents who cannot speak for themselves.

Give us speech, O God.

Give us ears to hear the cries of those creatures tortured in the name of science, skinned in the name of fashion, and neglected in the name of economy.

Let us hear their cries, O God.

Give us eyes to see our responsibilities, not just to the human community, but to the community of all living creatures. Let us be mindful of the rabbinic injunction that, 'The way a person treats an animal is an index to his soul.'

Help us to see, O God.

In this world so full of violence and unkindness, let us act in a gentle way towards all your creatures. A simple stroke on a dog's head, a scratch on a cat's chin, food for birds in winter and hunting with cameras only.

Help us to be gentle, O God.

Help us to lessen the suffering of your creatures, O God. Hasten the coming of your kingdom when the sun will shine on all your creation living in peace and love.

We pray all this, O Lord. Help us to be kind and gentle like our Lord Jesus. And may we remember St Francis' love of animals whenever we see one of your creatures hurt, suffering, and in need of help.

A Litany for Animals

4

Compassion

Readings
==

Balaam rose in the morning, and saddled his ass, and went with the princes of Moab. But God's anger was kindled because he went; and the angel of the Lord took his stand in the way as his adversary. Now he was riding on the ass, and his two servants were with him. And the ass saw the angel of the Lord standing in the road, with a drawn sword in his hand; and the ass turned aside out of the road, and went into the field; and Balaam struck the ass, to turn her into the road. Then the angel of the Lord stood in a narrow path between the vineyards, with a wall on either side. And when the ass saw the angel of the Lord, she pushed against the wall, and pressed Balaam's foot against the wall; so he struck her again. Then the angel of the Lord went ahead, and stood in a narrow place, where there was no way to turn either to the right or to the left. When the ass saw the angel of the Lord, she lay down under Balaam; and Balaam's anger was kindled, and he struck the ass with his staff. Then the Lord opened the mouth of the ass, and she said to Balaam, 'What have I done to you, that you have struck me these three times?' And Balaam said to the ass, 'Because you have made sport of me. I wish I had a sword in my hand, for then I would kill you.' And the ass said to Balaam, 'Am I not your ass, upon which you have ridden all your life long to this day? Was I ever accustomed to do so to you?' And he said, 'No.'

Then the Lord opened the eyes of Balaam, and he saw the angel of the Lord standing in the way, with his drawn sword in his hand; and he bowed his head, and fell on his face. And the angel of the Lord said to him, 'Why have you struck your ass these three times? Behold, I have come forth to withstand you, because your way is perverse before me; and the ass saw me, and turned aside before me these three times. If she had not turned aside from me, surely just now I would have slain you and let her live.'

Numbers 22.21–33

A righteous man has regard for the life of his beast, but the mercy of the wicked is cruel.

Proverbs 12.10

How the beasts groan!
    The herds of cattle are perplexed
because there is no pasture for them;
    even the flocks of sheep are dismayed.
'Fear not, O land;
    be glad and rejoice,
    for the Lord has done great things!
Fear not, you beasts of the field,
    for the pastures of the wilderness are green;
the tree bears its fruit,
    the fig tree and the vine give their full yield.'

Joel 1.18, 2.21–2

And the Lord said, 'You pity the plant, for which you did not labour, nor did you make it grow, which came into being in a night, and perished in a night. And should not I pity Nineveh, that great city, in which there are more than a hundred and twenty thousand persons who do not know their right hand from their left, and also much cattle?'

Jonah 4.10–11

Blessed are the merciful, for they shall obtain mercy.

Matthew 5.7

Holy people are most loving and gentle in their dealings with their fellows, and even with the lower animals: for this reason it was said that 'A righteous man is merciful to the life of his beast.'

Surely we ought to show kindness and gentleness to animals for many reasons and chiefly because they are of the same origin as ourselves.

St John Chrysostom

What is a charitable heart? It is a heart which is burning with love for the whole creation, for men, for the birds, for the beasts, for the demons – for all creatures. He who has such a heart cannot see or call to mind a creature without his eyes being filled with tears by reason of the immense compassion which seizes his heart; a heart which is softened and can no longer bear to see or learn from others of any suffering, even the smallest pain, being inflicted upon a creature. That is why such a man never ceases to pray also for the animals, for the enemies of truth, and for those who do him evil, that they may be preserved and purified. He will pray even for the reptiles, moved by the infinite pity which reigns in the hearts of those who are becoming united with God.

St Isaac the Syrian

Poor innocent little creatures [to animals bound for slaughter]: if you were reasoning beings and could speak you would curse us. For we are the cause of your death, and what have you done to deserve it?

St Richard of Chichester

Man may dismiss compassion from his heart,
But God will never. When He charged the Jew
To assist his foe's down-fallen beast to rise;
And when the bush-exploring boy, that seized
The young, to let the parent bird go free;
Proved He not plainly that his meaner works
Are yet his care, and have an interest all,
All, in the universal Father's love? . . .

I would not enter on my list of friends
(Though graced with polish'd manners and fine sense,
Yet wanting sensibility) the man
Who needlessly sets foot upon a worm.
An inadvertent step may crush the snail,
That crawls at evening in the public path;
But he that has humanity, forewarn'd,
Will tread aside, and let the reptile live.

William Cowper

Can I see another's woe,
And not be in sorrow too?
Can I see another's grief,
And not seek for kind relief?

Can I see a falling tear,
And not feel my sorrow's share?
Can a father see his child
Weep, nor be with sorrow filled?

Can a mother sit and hear,
An infant groan, an infant fear?
No, no, never can it be,
Never, never can it be!

And can he, who smiles on all,
Hear the wren with sorrows small,
Hear the small bird's grief and care,
Hear the woes that infants bear,

And not sit beside the nest
Pouring pity in their breast,
And not sit the cradle near
Weeping tear on infant's tear,

And not sit both night and day,
Wiping all our tears away?
Oh, no, never can it be,
Never, never can it be!

He doth give his joy to all,
He becomes an infant small.
He becomes a man of woe,
He doth feel the sorrow too.

Think not thou canst sigh a sigh,
And thy maker is not by;
Think not thou canst weep a tear,
And thy maker is not near.

Oh, he gives to us his joy
That our grief he may destroy;
Till our grief is fled and gone,
He doth sit by us and moan.

William Blake

We may pretend to what RELIGION we please; but
Cruelty is ATHEISM. We may make our boast of
CHRISTIANITY; but Cruelty is INFIDELITY. We
may trust to our ORTHODOXY; but Cruelty is the
worst of HERESIES.

Humphry Primatt

Think of your feelings at cruelty practised upon brute
animals and you will gain the sort of feeling which the
history of Christ's Cross and Passion ought to excite
within you.

Cardinal Newman

How can I teach your children gentleness,
And mercy to the weak, and reverence
For Life, which, in its weakness or excess,
Is still a gleam of God's omnipotence,
Or Death, which, seeming darkness, is no less
The self-same light, although averted hence,
When by your laws, your actions, and your speech,
You contradict the very things I teach?

Henry Wadsworth Longfellow

So zestfully canst thou sing?
And all this indignity,
With God's consent, on thee!
Blinded ere yet a-wing
By the red-hot needle thou,
I stand and wonder how
So zestfully thou canst sing!

Who hath charity? This bird.
Who suffereth long and is kind?
Is not provoked, though blind
And alive ensepulchred?
Who hopeth, endureth all things?
Who thinketh no evil, but sings?
Who is divine? This bird.

Thomas Hardy

I hear a sudden cry of pain!
There is a rabbit in a snare:
Now I hear the cry again,
But I cannot tell from where.

But I cannot tell from where
He is calling out for aid;
Crying on the frightened air,
Making everything afraid.

Making everything afraid,
Wrinkling up his little face,
As he cries again for aid;
And I cannot find the place!

And I cannot find the place
Where his paw is in the snare:
Little one! Oh, little one!
I am searching everywhere.

James Stephens

Cries are still heard in secret nooks,
Till hushed with gag or slit or thud:
And hideous dens whereon none looks
Are sprayed with needless blood.
But here, in battlings, patient, slow,
Much has been won – more, maybe, than we know –
And on we labour hopeful. 'Ailinon!'
A mighty voice calls: 'But may the good prevail!'
And 'Blessed are the merciful!'
Calls a yet mightier one.

Thomas Hardy

He bears in his heart all wounds . . .
The wounds of the baited bear –
The blind and weeping bear whom the keepers beat
On his helpless flesh . . . the tears of the hunted hare.

Edith Sitwell

A man is truly ethical only when he obeys the compulsion to help all life which he is able to assist, and shrinks from injuring anything that lives. He does not ask how far this or that life deserves one's sympathy as being valuable, nor, beyond that, whether and to what degree it is capable of feeling. Life as such is sacred to him. He tears no leaf from a tree, plucks no flower, and takes care to crush no insect. If in summer he is working by lamplight, he prefers to keep the window shut and breathe a stuffy atmosphere rather than to see one insect after another fall with singed wings to the ground.

Albert Schweitzer

Prayers

===

May my soul always find fulfilment
In friendship towards all beings,
In happiness, in the goodness of men,
In compassion towards all suffering creatures.
May my feelings be neutral towards the hostile.
This is my prayer.

Tiruvalluvan

O merciful Father, who hast given life to all things, and lovest all that thou hast made, pour into the hearts of men the spirit of thy own loving kindness, that they may show mercy to helpless creatures and glorify thee by that gentleness which is in accordance with thy holy will.

William Marlborough Carter

Hear our humble prayer, O God, for our friends the animals, Thy creatures. In Thy hand is the soul of every living thing, and we bless Thee that Thou carest for the dumb creatures of the earth. We bless and praise Thee for Thy joy in their beauty and grace, and we desire to share Thy love for them all.

Accept our prayer especially for animals who are suffering; for all that are over-worked and under-fed and cruelly treated; for all wistful creatures in captivity, which beat against the bars; for any that are hunted or lost or deserted or frightened or hungry; for all that are in pain or dying; for all that must be put to death. We entreat for them all Thy *mercy and pity, and for those who deal with them we ask a heart of compassion, and gentle hands, and kindly words.*

Make us ourselves to be true friends to animals and so to share the blessings of the merciful, for the sake of Thy Son, the Tenderhearted, Jesus Christ our Lord.

Rodborough Bede Book

O Lamb of God, Who trembled in the cold
Under the slicing sharpness of the snows,
Be mindful of the knifed and quivering flesh
Of tortured animals, and of all those
That, living sacrifices of man's power,
Die in unutterable throes.

Liam Brophy

O God, who hast made all the earth
and every creature that dwells therein:
Help us, we pray thee,
to treat with compassion
the living creatures entrusted to our care,
that they may not suffer from our neglect
nor become the victims of any cruelty;
and grant that in caring for them
we may find a deeper understanding
of thy love for all creation;
through Jesus Christ our Lord.

Source unknown

O Lord our God,
who hatest nothing that thou
   hast made,
keep us from all cruelty
   to beasts, birds
   or any of thy creatures.
May we always remember that thou
   hast made both them and us,
and show them the mercy
   that we have received
   from thee;
   for thy Name's sake.

Source unknown

We call upon Thy mercy, O Lord,
without ceasing:
grant that these animals,
afflicted with grievous disease,
may be restored to health
in Thy name
and by the power of Thy blessing.
May all the power of the devil
be driven from them
so that they will languish no more.
Be Thou, O Lord,
the protector of their lives
and the healer of their bodies.

From the Rituale Romanum

Unto God's gracious mercy and protection we commit you, the Lord bless and keep you, the Lord make His face to shine upon you and give you a caring heart, and upon animals here, the animals in the fields, the birds around us, and the fish in the seas and streams, may you be blessed in the name of God your Holy Creator.

Source unknown

O God, whose name is Love, you created this world and all that is in it. We ask you to look with compassion and mercy upon us all. Look upon your wild creatures, O God, which delight us by their variety and beauty. Be with them in their struggle for existence, and shelter them from the natural and man-made dangers which surround them.

Lord in your mercy, hear our prayer.

Look upon the companion animals, O God, which share our homes and our lives, and which show us a love and loyalty few men can surpass. Bless them for the pleasure and companionship they give, and protect all those who suffer neglect and cruelty.

Lord in your mercy, hear our prayer.

Look especially, O God, upon all those your creatures which suffer at the hands of man in laboratories, intensive farms, abattoirs, traps, sport and entertainment. Be with them in their fear, pain and suffering, and hold them in your loving hands.

Lord in your mercy, hear our prayer.

Look upon man, O God, your supreme creation, with love and mercy. Forgive us our selfishness and our cruelty and lead us gently back into your way of love. Transform our hearts until they truly reflect the way shown to us by your beloved Son, Jesus Christ, whose love was perfect and who loved to the end that he gave his own life for us.

Lord in your mercy, hear our prayer.

Forgive us our bitterness against those who abuse your creation, for Christ taught us to forgive, even as he forgave. Yet change the hearts of all who use animals with cruelty so that they may be filled with your love and mercy. Inspire all Governments, and those in authority, to change the directions of medical research and food production, and to bring an end by law to all animal abuse.

Lord in your mercy, hear our prayer.

Guide us all by your Holy Spirit into his transforming way of truth and love, and nurture in us a Christ-like spirit of compassion which is boundless and perfect.
O God, we await the coming of your Kingdom, in our hearts and in your world.

Merciful Father, accept these prayers for the sake of your Son, our Saviour Jesus Christ.   Amen.

May Tripp

5

Redemption

Readings

===

The wolf shall dwell with the lamb,
   and the leopard shall lie down with the kid,
and the calf and the lion and the fatling together,
   and a little child shall lead them.
The cow and the bear shall feed;
   their young shall lie down together;
   and the lion shall eat straw like the ox.
The suckling child shall play over the hole of the
     asp,
   and the weaned child shall put his hand on the
     adder's den.
They shall not hurt or destroy
   in all my holy mountain;
for the earth shall be full of the knowledge of the
     Lord
   as the waters cover the sea.

Isaiah 11.6–9

Behold the Lord God comes with might,
   and his arm rules for him;
behold his reward is with him,
   and his recompense before him.
He will feed his flock like a shepherd,
   he will gather the lambs in his arms,
he will carry them in his bosom,
   and gently lead those that are with young.

Isaiah 40.10–11

And I will make for you a covenant on that day with the beasts of the field, the birds of the air, and the creeping things of the ground; and I will abolish the bow, the sword, and war from the land; and I will make you lie down in safety.

Hosea 2.18

Man and beast thou savest, O Lord.

Psalm 36.6b

He is the image of the invisible God, the first-born of all creation; for in him all things were created, in heaven and on earth, visible and invisible, whether thrones or dominions or principalities or authorities – all things were created through him and for him. He is before all things, and in him all things hold together. He is the head of the body, the church; he is the beginning, the first-born from the dead, that in everything he might be pre-eminent. For in him all the fullness of God was pleased to dwell, and through him to reconcile to himself all things, whether on earth or in heaven, making peace by the blood of his cross.

Colossians 1.15–20

I consider that the sufferings of this present time are not worth comparing with the glory that is to be revealed to us. For the creation waits with eager longing for the revealing of the sons of God; for the creation was subjected to futility, not of its own will but by the will of him who subjected it in hope; because the creation itself will be set free from its bondage to decay and obtain the glorious liberty of the children of God. We know that the whole creation has been groaning in travail together until now; and not only the creation, but we ourselves, who have the first fruits of the Spirit, groan inwardly as we wait for adoption as sons, the redemption of our bodies.

Romans 8.18–23

I am concerned that God stores up and keeps by Himself much greater visions than the sun, the moon, and the chorus of stars have seen, indeed than the holy angels have seen, whom God made wind and a flame of fire [cf. Psalm 104.4; Hebrews 1.7]. His purpose is to reveal them when the whole creation is set free from its bondage to the Enemy for the glorious liberty of the children of God.

Origen

When the Word visited the holy Virgin Mary, the Spirit came to her with him, and the Word in the Spirit moulded the body and conformed it to himself, desiring to join and present all creation to the Father through himself, and in it to reconcile all things, having made peace, whether things in heaven or things upon the earth.

St Athanasius

The great Son is the glory of the Father
and shone out from him like light . . .
He assumed a body
to bring help to suffering creatures . . .
He was sacrifice and celebrant,
sacrificial priest and God himself.
He offered blood to God to cleanse the entire world.

St Gregory Nazianzen

He [the Holy Spirit] is supremely Great Power, divine and unsearchable, living and rational, and it belongs to him to sanctify all things that were made by God through Christ . . . It is the Holy Spirit who knows the mysteries, searching all things, even the depths of God . . . For there is one God . . . one Lord . . . and one Holy Spirit who has power to sanctify and deify all, who spoke in the Law and the Prophets, in the Old and New Testaments alike.

St Cyril of Jerusalem

And not only did [God] communicate to them their being and their natural graces when He beheld them, as we have said, but also in this image of His Son alone He left them clothed with beauty, communicating to them supernatural being. This was when He became man, and thus exalted man in the beauty of God, and consequently exalted the creatures in him, since in uniting Himself with man He united Himself with the nature of them all . . .

And thus in this lifting up of the Incarnation of His Son, and in the glory of His resurrection according to the flesh, not only did the Father beautify the creatures in part, but we can say that He left them all clothed with beauty and dignity.

St John of the Cross

Why are we by all creatures waited on?
Why do the prodigal elements supply
Life and food to me, being more pure than I,
Simple, and further from corruption?
Why brook'st thou, ignorant horse, subjection?
Why dost thou bull, and boar so sillily
Dissemble weakness, and by one man's stroke die,
Whose whole kind, you might swallow and feed
    upon?
Weaker I am, woe is me, and worse than you,
You have not sinned, nor need be timorous.
But wonder at a greater wonder, for to us
Created nature doth these things subdue,
But their Creator, whom sin, nor nature tied,
For us, his creatures, and his foes, hath died.

John Donne

Ah, poor companion! when thou followed last
Thy master's parting footsteps to the gate
Which closed for ever on him, thou didst lose
Thy best friend, and none was left to plead
For the old age of brute fidelity.
But fare thee well. Mine is no narrow creed,
And He who gave thee being did not frame
The mystery of life to be the sport
Of merciless men. There is another world
For all that live and move – a better one!
Where the proud bipeds, who would fain confine
Infinite goodness to the little bounds
Of their own charity, may envy thee.

Robert Southey

The whole brute creation will then, undoubtedly, be restored not only to the vigour, strength, and swiftness which they had at their creation, but to a far higher degree of each than they ever enjoyed . . . Thus, in that day, all the vanity to which they are helplessly subject will be abolished; they will suffer no more, either from within or without; the days of their groaning are ended.

John Wesley

But is it true that Death is the lord of any man or woman or child; of any beast or any insect; of any tree or flower? No. Death did not make them; and He who did make them, He who gave them life, He by whom their life has been renewed every hour, He has proved that He is stronger than Death . . . We wait for the Deliverer of these bodies from their aches and torments; we wait for the day when Christ shall set them free from the bondage of death; when He shall make them like his glorious body. And as we hope for ourselves, so we hope for all those creatures who not for their own fault have been made subject to misery and death, who are not sinful as we have been.

F. D. Maurice

Thank Him because He has said there will be a day in which He will gather up all things unto Christ, both things in heaven and things on earth, unto Him who is the Head over all His universe; and when every child, and every star, and every animal, and every flower, shall be seen to have been created by infinite love for His infinite glory.

F. D. Maurice

Oh yet we trust that somehow good
Will be the final goal of ill,
To pangs of nature, sins of will,
Defects of doubt, and taints of blood;

That nothing walks with aimless feet;
That not one life shall be destroy'd,
Or cast as rubbish to the void,
When God hath made the pile complete;

That not a worm is cloven in vain;
That not a moth with vain desire
Is shrivell'd in a fruitless fire,
Or but subserves another's gain.

Behold, we know not anything;
I can but trust that good shall fall
At last – far off – at last to all,
And every winter change to spring.

Alfred Lord Tennyson

In his way to union with God, man in no way leaves
creatures aside, but gathers together in his love the
whole cosmos disordered by sin, that it may at last be
transfigured by grace.

Vladimir Lossky

Christ is the new creature . . . Nature is not
reconciled, like man and history, but it is redeemed
for a new freedom . . . In the sacrament, Christ is the
mediator between nature and God, and stands for all
creatures before God.

Dietrich Bonhoeffer

Prayers

The whole creation
was altered by thy Passion;
for all things suffered
with thee,
knowing, O Lord,
that thou holdest all things
in unity.

From the Byzantine Rite

For those, O Lord,
the humble beasts,
that bear with us
the burden and heat of the day,
and offer their guileless lives
for the well-being of humankind;
and for the wild creatures,
whom Thou hast made
wise, strong, and beautiful,
we supplicate for them
Thy great tenderness of heart,
for Thou hast promised to save
both man and beast,
and great is Thy loving kindness,
O Master,
Saviour of the world.

St Basil the Great

O knowing, glorious Spirit, when
Thou shalt restore trees, beasts and men,
when Thou shalt make all new again,
destroying only death and pain,
give him amongst Thy works a place,
who in them loved and sought Thy face.

Henry Vaughan

Lord God,
no flash of beauty,
no enchantment of goodness,
no element of force,
but finds in you
the ultimate refinement
and consummation of itself.

Eternal Father,
who through Jesus Christ,
our ascending Lord,
sent your Holy Spirit
to be the bond of fellowship
in the Church:
unify the whole created order
in Christ;
who reigns supreme
over all things
with you and the same Spirit,
one God,
for ever and ever.

From A Christian's Prayer Book

Almighty God,
whose glory the heavens
* are telling,*
who art the breath of life
* of all living things:*
To thee be praise
from all thy creatures,
and from man,
*   made in thine own image,*
*   redeemed and restored*
*   by Jesus Christ*
*   thine only Son,*
*   our Lord,*
Amen.

From the RSPCA Order of Service

May Almighty God
Father, Son and Holy Spirit,
bless these animals,
protect them from all cruelty
and grant them with us
a share in the redemption
of your creation.

From the RSPCA Order of Service

God of everlasting love,
who is eternally forgiving,
pardon and restore us,
and make us one with you
in your new creation.
Amen.

From the RSPCA Order of Service

Lord of all life
your creation groans in travail
awaiting the sons of God;
by your Spirit help us
to free creation
from its bondage,
to heal its pain
and obtain that liberty
which is your gift to all creatures.

Holy Father
your Son, Jesus Christ
is the reconciler of all things
in heaven and on earth;
send us your Spirit
that we may be made one
with all your creatures,
and know that all things
come from you,
through you,
and belong to you
now and forever.

From the RSPCA Order of Service

Christ Jesus,
You are the beginning and the end.
In you all things were created
    and in you all things are redeemed.

Christ Jesus,
You are Lord of creation.
It was for all that you gave your life
    on the cross, a perfect sacrifice.

Take now, to your open arms,
*   our grief for your creation:*
for your wildlife, struggling against extinction;
for the hunted and the trapped;
for the abandoned and the homeless;
for your food animals, unnaturally imprisoned,
*   transported and slaughtered in terror;*
for your animals cruelly used as
*   laboratory tools.*

Christ Jesus,
In us you live as Risen Lord.
Our hearts plead with you now to carry the
*   pain of your suffering creatures,*
*   even to the least of these.*
The darkness of the world binds them
*   as it binds us, O Lord,*
and only your love can free us to live
*   in your light.*

Christ Jesus, come.
Redeem your world.
Amen.

May Tripp

Guide to Educational Resources

Publications

ON RELIGIOUS/THEOLOGICAL ASPECTS

Agius, Ambrose, *God's Animals*, foreword by Cardinal Heenan (London, Catholic Study Circle for Animal Welfare, 1970).

Allchin, A. M., *Wholeness and Transfiguration Illustrated in the Lives of St Francis of Assisi and St Seraphim of Sarov* (Oxford, SLG Press, 1974).

Carpenter, Edward and others, *Animals and Ethics* (London, Element Books, 1980).

Cobb Jr., John, *Is It Too Late? A Theology of Ecology* (Beverley Hills, California, Bruce, 1972).

Granberg-Michaelson, Wesley (ed.), *Tending the Garden: Essays on the Gospel and the Earth* (Grand Rapids, Michigan, Eerdmans, 1987).

Hart, John, *The Spirit of the Earth: A Theology of the Land* (New Jersey, Paulist Press, 1984).

Hendry, George S., *Theology of Nature* (Philadelphia, Westminster Press, 1980).

Hume, C. W., *The Status of Animals in the Christian Religion* (London, Universities Federation for Animal Welfare, 1957).

Linzey, Andrew, *The Status of Animals in the Christian Tradition* (Birmingham, Woodbrooke College, 1985).
Christianity and the Rights of Animals (London, SPCK, 1987).
(ed. with Tom Regan), *Animals and Christianity: A Book of Readings* (London, SPCK, 1988).
(ed. with Tom Regan), *The Song of Creation: Poetry in Celebration of Animals* (Basingstoke, Marshall Pickering, 1988).

McDonagh, Sean, *To Care for the Earth: A Call to a New Theology* (Dublin, Geoffrey Chapman, 1986).

Moltmann, Jürgen, *God in Creation: An Ecological Doctrine of Creation* (London, SCM Press, 1985).

Montefiore, Hugh (ed.), *Man and Nature* (London, Collins, 1975).

Regan, Tom (ed.), *Animal Sacrifices: Religious Perspectives on the Use of Animals in Science*, introduction by John Bowker (Philadelphia, Temple University Press, 1986).

Santmire, Paul H., *The Travail of Nature: The Ambiguous Ecological Promise of Christian Theology* (Philadelphia, Fortress Press, 1985).

Schweitzer, Albert, *Civilization and Ethics* (London, Allen and Unwin, 1933).

Seraphim, Sister, *All God's Creatures* (London, William Kimber, 1976).

Torrance, T. F., *Divine and Contingent Order* (Oxford, Oxford University Press, 1981).

Wynne-Tyson, Jon, *The Extended Circle: A Dictionary of Humane Thought* (Fontwell, Sussex, Centaur Press, 1986).

ON PHILOSOPHICAL ASPECTS

Attfield, Robin, *The Ethics of Environmental Concern* (Oxford, Basil Blackwell, 1983).

Clark, Stephen R. L., *The Moral Status of Animals* (Oxford, Clarendon Press, 1977).

Godlovitch, Stanley and Rosalind, and Harris, John (eds.), *Animals, Men and Morals: An Enquiry into the Maltreatment of Non-Humans* (London, Victor Gollancz, 1971).

Magel, Charles R., *Key Guide to Information Sources in Animal Rights* (London and New York, Mansell), 1988).

Midgley, Mary, *Animals and Why They Matter: A Journey Around the Species Barrier* (Harmondsworth, Penguin Books, 1983).

Miller, H. and Williams, W. (eds.), *Ethics and Animals* (New Jersey, Humana Press, 1983).

Regan, Tom, *All That Dwell Therein: Essays on Animal Rights and Environmental Ethics* (Berkeley, California, University of California Press, 1982).

The Case for Animal Rights (Berkeley, California, University of California Press, 1983).

(ed. with Peter Singer), *Animal Rights and Human Obligations* (New Jersey, Prentice-Hall, 1976).

Singer, Peter, *Animal Liberation: A New Ethic for our Treatment of Animals* (London, Jonathan Cape, 1976).

ON SPECIALIST TOPICS

Jordan, Bill and Ormrod, Stefan, *The Last Great Wild Beast Show: A Discussion on the Failure of British Animal Collections* (London, Constable, 1978).

McKenna, Virginia, Travers, Will and Wray, Jonathan (eds.), *Beyond the Bars: the Zoo Dilemma* (Wellingborough, Thorsons, 1987).

Mason, James and Singer, Peter, *Animal Factories* (New York, Crown, 1980).

Paterson, David (ed.), *Humane Education – A Symposium* (Sussex, Humane Education Council, 1981).

Ryder, R. D., *Victims of Science: The Use of Animals in Research* (London, National Anti-Vivisection Society, 1983).

Singer, Peter (ed.), *In Defence of Animals* (Oxford, Basil Blackwell, 1986).

Sperlinger, David (ed.), *Animals in Research* (London, John Wiley and Sons, 1980).

Townend, Christine, *Pulling the Wool: A New Look at the Australian Wool Industry* (Sydney, Hales and Iremonger, 1985).

Films, Videos and Tapes

For a complete list of audio-visual aids (including films, wall charts and educational packs) contact the Education Department of the RSPCA (Causeway, Horsham, West Sussex RH12 1HG, UK) or the Humane Society of the United States (2100 L. Street N.W., Washington DC, USA).

In addition, the Christian Education Movement (2 Chester House, Pages Lane, London N10 1PR, UK) produce an educational pack for secondary schools entitled *Animals and Religion*.

The Rights of Animals: A Comprehensive Guide to the Debate about Animals (1987). 3 × 40-minute audio tapes on all aspects of animal welfare from a religious and philosophical standpoint, and a study guide, by Andrew Linzey, Tom Regan and Peter Elvy. Distributed in the UK by Ecuvision (10–12 High Street, Great Wakering, Essex SS3 0EQ).

We Are All Noah (1985). A 40-minute video on Jewish and Christian attitudes towards animals suitable for sixth formers in the UK and High School students in the US, as well as adult Christian groups. Written and directed by Tom Regan and produced by Kay Reibold. Distributed in the UK by Ecuvision (address above), and in the US by the Culture and Animals Foundation (3509 Eden Croft Drive, Raleigh, NC 27612, USA).

The Animals Film (1982). The first comprehensive film documentary on animal abuse. Produced and directed by Victor Schonfeld and Myriam Alaux. 136 minutes. Distributed in the USA by Pyramid Films, New York, and in the UK by Concord Films Ltd (201 Felixstowe Road, Ipswich, Suffolk IP3 9BJ).

Rabbits Don't Cry (1983). A documentary originally produced by BBC TV on the ethics of animal experimentation. Commentary by Richard Adams and others. 40 minutes. Distributed in the UK by Concord Films Ltd (address above).

No Treats for Animals (1984). A film made for 8–13-year-old children, aiming to raise appropriate questions for this age range. Sponsored by Animal Aid. 16 minutes. Distributed in the UK by Concord Films Ltd (address above).

What Price Beauty? (1977). A film specifically made for Beauty Without Cruelty, highlighting the plight of animals killed or confined in cramped quarters for the production of furs and cosmetics. Commentary by Tony Britten and Rolf Harris. 30 minutes. Distributed in the UK by Concord Films Ltd (address above).

Don't Look Now – Here Comes your Dinner (1973). A film on factory farming raising both ethical and agricultural questions – for example, can producing grain for animal feed be a right use of world resources? Sponsored by Compassion in World Farming. 35 minutes. Distributed in the UK by Concord Films Ltd (address above).

Diet for a Small Planet (1974). A film offering a radical review of farming practices. The case against meat-eating on ethical, economical and nutritional grounds is expounded. 28 minutes. Produced by Bullfrog Productions, USA, and distributed in the UK by Concord Films Ltd (address above).

Organizations

SPECIFICALLY CHRISTIAN ORGANIZATIONS

Christian Consultative Council for Animal Welfare
Chaired by the former Dean of Westminster, this council co-ordinates the work of all the Christian animal societies in the UK. It also produces policy statements and prayer leaflets. Secretary: Mrs J. Watson, 23 Ravensbourne Road, London SE6, UK.

Christian Ecology Group
Concerned to foster greater understanding of Christian insights into the Green Movement. It produces a regular newsletter. Secretary: Judith Pritchard, 58 Quest Hills Road, Malvern, Worcs. WR14 1RW, UK.

Anglican Society for the Welfare of Animals
Works specifically for members of the Church of England but membership is open to all Christians. It produces a regular bulletin and other literature. Secretary: Valerie Elliott, 10 Chester Avenue, Hawkenbury, Tunbridge Wells, Kent, UK.

Catholic Study Circle for Animal Welfare
Especially represents Roman Catholics but again membership is open to all Christians. It produces a regular journal called *The Ark*. Free copy on request to the Secretary: May Bocking, 39 Onslow Gardens, South Woodford, London E18, UK.

Quaker Concern for Animal Welfare
Helps co-ordinate concern among members of the Society of Friends. Free literature from the Secretary: Angela Howard, Webb's Cottage, Saling, Braintree, Essex CM7 5DZ, UK.

Animal Christian Concern

An ecumenical group holding an annual service in one of the cathedrals and producing a regular journal, *ACC News*. Secretary: May Tripp, 46 St Margaret's Road, Horsford, Leeds LS18 5BG, UK.

Willow Tree Sanctuary for Animal Welfare

A modern sanctuary inspired by Christian ideals and working generally for greater Christian understanding of animals. Secretary: Pamela Townsend, Willow Tree Sanctuary, Gainsford End, Nr. Toppesfield, Halstead, Essex, UK.

St Francis Trust

Inspired by St Francis and St Seraphim; works towards a holistic vision of creation. For more information contact: Jeanne Knights, c/o 28 Warwick Road, Thorpe Bay, Essex, UK.

Christians Helping Animals and People Inc.

An ecumenical organization concerned to show how Christian ministry should extend to all creatures. Produces a regular newsletter entitled 'CHAPter'. Contact: Frances Arnetta, CHAP, PO Box 272, Selden, New York 11784, USA.

International Network for Religion and Animals

An international forum for the exchange of news and views on religious approaches to animals. Contact: Dr Michael Fox, PO Box 33061, Washington DC, 20033–0061, USA.

Task Force on Religion and Animal Rights

An organization dedicated to the furtherance of animal rights within differing religious traditions. Chairman: Alec B. Kyle, 234 Fountainville Center, Fountainville, PA 18923, USA.

The International Society for Religion and Animal Rights (ISRAR)
ISRAR is feminist, holistic and committed to social justice and peace for all life forms on the planet. Founder and Director: Joan Beth Clair, 1798 Scenic Avenue, Berkeley, CA 94709, USA.

GENERAL AND SPECIALIST ORGANIZATIONS

American Anti-Vivisection Society
Suite 204 Noble Plaza, 801 Old York Road, Jenkintown, PA 19046–1685, USA

American Vegan Society
PO Box H, Malaga, New Jersey 08328, USA

American Vegetarians
Box 5424, Akron, Ohio 44313, USA

Animal Aid
7 Castle Street, Tonbridge, Kent TN9 1BH, UK

Animal Defence League of Canada
PO Box 3880, Station C, Ottawa, Ontario K1Y 4M5, Canada

Animal Liberation Inc.
319 West 74th Street, New York, NY 10023, USA

Animal Protection Association
1 Claremont, Newlaithes Road, Leeds LS18 4LG, UK

Animal Rights Association
18 Annandale Road, London SE10 0DA, UK

Animals' Vigilantes
James Mason House, 24 Salisbury Street, Fordingbridge, Hants SP6 1AF, UK

Animal Welfare Institute
PO Box 3650, Washington DC 20007, USA

Argus Archives
228 East 49th Street, New York, NY 10017, USA

Australians for Animals
Box C616, Clarence St Post Office, Sydney 2000,
Australia

Beauty Without Cruelty
175 West 12th Street, New York, NY 10017, USA;
37 Avebury Avenue, Tonbridge, Kent TN9 1TL, UK

British League for Animal Rights
5 Aysgarth Road, Dulwich Village, London SE21
7JR, UK

British Union for the Abolition of Vivisection
16a Crane Grove, London N7 8LB, UK

*British Veterinary Association Animal Welfare
Foundation* (BVA–AWF)
7 Mansfield Street, London W1M 0AT, UK

Campaign Against Farm Animal Abuse
54 Allison Street, Digbeth, Birmingham 5, UK

Captive Animals Protection Society
17 Raphael Road, Hove, Sussex BN3 5QP, UK

Care for the Wild
2 North Holmes Close, Roffey, Horsham,
West Sussex, UK

Cats Protection League
20 North Street, Horsham, West Sussex RH12 1BN,
UK

Chicken's Lib
6 Pilling Lane, Skelmanthorpe, Huddersfield, West
Yorks, UK

Compassion for Animals Foundation
Box 5312 Beverly Hills, California 90210, USA

Compassion in World Farming
20 Lavant Street, Petersfield, Hants GU32 5EW, UK

Crusade Against All Cruelty to Animals
Humane Education Centre, Avenue Lodge,
Bounds Green Lane, London N22 4EU, UK

Culture and Animals Foundation
Eden Croft, Raleigh, North Carolina 27612, USA

Dr Hadwyn Trust for Humane Research
46 King's Road, Hitchin, Herts SG5 1RD, UK

Farm and Food Society
4 Willifield Way, London NW11 7XT, UK

Fight Animal Cruelty Everywhere (FACE)
Danbury View, Peverel Avenue, Nounsley, Hatfield
Peverel, Chelmsford, Essex CM3 2NA, UK

Friends of Animals Inc.
11 West 60th Street, New York, NY 10023, USA, and
2712 Seaview Road, Victoria, BC V8N 1K7, Canada

Friends of the Earth
377 City Road, London EC1V 1NA, UK

The Fund for Animals
140 West 47th Street, New York, NY 10019, USA,
and 12548 Ventura Blvd., Ste 141, Studio City, California 91604, USA

Greenpeace Ltd
36 Graham Street, London N1 8LL, UK

Humane Research Trust
29 Bramhall Lane, South Bramhall, Stockport,
Cheshire SK7 2DN, UK

Humane Society of the United States (HSUS)
2100 L. Street, Washington DC, USA

International Association Against Painful Experiments on Animals
PO Box 215, St Albans, Herts AL3 4RD, UK

International Council Against Bull-Fighting
13 Graystone Road, Tenterden, Kent CT5 2JY, UK

International Fund for Animal Welfare
Tubwell House, New Road, Crowborough, East Sussex TN6 2HQ, UK

International League for the Protection of Horses
PO Box 166, 67a Camden High Street, London NW1 7JL, UK

International Primate Protection League
19–25 Argyll Street, London W1V 2DU, UK

International Society for Animal Rights
421 South State Street, Clarks Summit, PA 18411, USA

Laboratory Animals Protection Society
Park Cottage, Redenham, Nr Andover, Hampshire, UK

League Against Cruel Sports
83–87 Union Street, London SE1 1SG, UK

Lifeforce
Box 3117, Main Post Office, Vancouver, BC, Canada

LYNX
PO Box 509, Great Dunmow, Essex CM6 1UH, UK

National Anti-Vivisection Society
51 Harley Street, London W1N 1DD, UK

National Anti-Vivisection Society (U.S.)
53 West Jackson Boulevard, Suite 1550, Chicago, IL
60604, USA

National Dog Rescue
The Crippetts, Jordans, Beaconsfield, Bucks, UK

National Society for the Abolition of Cruel Sports
Freepost, Forest Row, East Sussex RH18 5ZA, UK

New England Anti-Vivisection Society
333 Washington Street, Suite 850, Boston, MA 02108,
USA

People's Trust for Endangered Species
19 Quarry Street, Guildford, Surrey GU1 3EH, UK

PRO DOGS
203 London Road, Aylesford, Kent ME20 7PZ, UK

Protect Our Livestock
10 Pilford Avenue, Cheltenham, Glos., UK

RSPCA
Causeway, Horsham, West Sussex RH12 1HG, UK

Scottish Anti-Vivisection Society
121 West Regent Street, Glasgow G2 2SD, UK

Scottish Society for the Prevention of Vivisection
10 Queensferry Street, Edinburgh EH2 4PG, UK

Sea Shepherd Fund
12 Royal Terrace, Glasgow G3 7NY, UK

United Action for Animals
205 East 42nd Street, New York, NY 10017, USA

Universities Federation for Animal Welfare
8 Hamilton Close, South Mimms, UK

Vegan Society
33–35 George Street, Oxford OX1 2AY, UK

Vegetarian Society UK Ltd
Parkdale, Dunham Road, Altrincham, Cheshire WA14 4QG, UK

World Society for the Protection of Animals
106 Jermyn Street, London SW1Y 6EE, UK, and 29 Perkins Street, PO Box 190, Boston, Mass. 02130, USA

Zoo Check
Cherry Tree Cottage, Coldharbour, Dorking, Surrey RH5 6HA

Notes on Sources

All biblical references are from the Revised Standard Version (RSV).

I CREATION

Page

7 **Tertullian** (*c*.160–*c*.230). 'On Prayer', ch. 29, extract in Brother Kenneth CGA (ed.), *From the Fathers to the Churches* (London, Collins, 1983).

8 **St Athanasius** (*c*. 296–373). *Contra Gentes and De Incarnatione*, ed. and tr. R. W. Thomson (Oxford, Clarendon Press, 1971).

8 **St Gregory of Nyssa** (*c*. 335–*c*. 395). 'Address on Religious Instruction' in E. R. Hardy and C. C. Richardson (eds.), *Christology of the Later Fathers*, vol. iii (London, SCM Press, 1964).

9 **St Augustine of Hippo** (354–430). *City of God*, Book XII, 4 and 5.

9 **St Bonaventure** (1221–1274). *The Soul's Journey into God*, tr. and intro. by Ewert Cousins, Classics of Western Spirituality (London, SPCK, 1979).

10 **Julian of Norwich** (*c*. 1360–?). *Showings*, tr. and intro. by Edmund Colledge and James Walsh, Classics of Western Spirituality (London, SPCK, 1979).

10 **Thomas à Kempis** (1379–1471). 'The Imitation of Christ' cited in Jon Wynne-Tyson (ed.), *The Extended Circle: A Dictionary of Humane Thought* (Fontwell, Sussex, Centaur Press, 1985).

10 **William Wordsworth** (1770–1850). From 'Lines Composed a Few Miles above Tintern Abbey, on Revisiting the Banks of the Wye during a Tour, July 13, 1798' in David Wright (ed.), *Penguin Book of English Romantic Verse* (Harmondsworth, Penguin Books, 1970).

11 **John Clare** (1793–1864). From 'Nature's Hymn to Deity' in J. W. Tibbie (ed.), *Selected Poems* (London, J. M. Dent, 1976).

11 **John Hampden Gurney** (1802–1862). From 'Yes – God is Good in Earth and Sky' in *The Methodist Hymn-Book* (London, Methodist Conference Office, 1954).

11 **Ralph Waldo Emerson** (1803–1882). From 'Woodnotes' in *Poems* (London, Routledge and Sons, no date).

12 **F. D. Maurice** (1805–1872). 'The Gift of Hearing' in *Sermons Preached in Country Churches*, 2nd edn. (London, Macmillan, 1880).

12 **Fyodor Mikhail Dostoevsky** (1821–1881). *The Brothers Karamazov*, tr. by David Magarshack, vol. i (Harmondsworth, Penguin Books, 1969).

12 **Austin Farrer** (1906–1968). *Love Almighty and Ills Unlimited* (London, Fontana, 1966).

13 **Christina Rossetti** (1803–1894). From 'To What Purpose This Waste?' cited in Jon Wynne-Tyson (ed.), op. cit.

13 **Gerard Manley Hopkins** (1844–1889). From 'God's Grandeur' in W. H. Gardner (ed.), *Poems and Prose* (Harmondsworth, Penguin Books, 1953).

14 **St Gregory Nazianzen** (c. 330–389). From 'Hymn to God' in *Selected Poems*, tr. and intro. by John McGuckin (Oxford, SLG Press, 1986).

15 **St Francis of Assisi** (c. 1181–1226). *The Mirror of Perfection*, intro. by Hugh McKay and postscript by Eric Doyle (London, J. M. Dent, 1963).

16 **The Book of Common Prayer** (1662). From the Benedicite, Omnia Opera, from Morning Prayer in *The Book of Common Prayer* (London, SPCK and Cambridge, Cambridge University Press, 1961).

17 **Isaac Watts** (1674–1748). From 'I Sing the Almighty Power of God' in *Congregational Praise*, 6th edn. (London, Independent Press, 1958).

17 **William Henry Draper** (1855–1933). Based on St Francis of Assisi, in *Congregational Praise*, 6th edn. (London, Independent Press, 1958).

18 **Charles Tennyson Turner** (1808–1879). 'Silent Praise' in John Betjeman and Charles Tennyson (eds.), *A Hundred Sonnets* (London, Rupert Hart-Davis, 1960).

18 **Robert Seymour Bridges** (1884–1930). From 'My Soul, Praise the Lord!' by William Kethe (fifteenth century) and revised by Bridges in *The Methodist Hymn-Book* (London, Methodist Conference Office, 1954).

19 **T. S. Eliot** (1888–1965). *Murder in the Cathedral* (London, Faber and Faber, 1969).

19 **W. H. Auden** (1907–1973). 'Anthem' in Peter Levi (ed.), *Penguin Book of Christian Verse* (Harmondsworth, Penguin Books, 1985).

20 **George Appleton** (1902–). From George Appleton (ed.), *The Oxford Book of Prayer* (Oxford, Oxford University Press, 1985).

20 **The Earth Mass** (1986). From the Liturgy of the Earth Mass on the Solemnity of St Francis, 5 October 1986, Cathedral Church of St John the Divine, New York.

2 COMMUNION

26 **St Guthlac of Crowland** (*c.* 673–714). Cited in La Marquise de Rambures, *L'Église et la Pitié Envers les Animaux* (Paris 1908) and in A. Agius, *God's Animals* (London, Catholic Study Circle for Animal Welfare, 1970).

26 **St Godric of Finchale** (*c.* 1065–1170). From Butler's *Lives of the Saints* cited in A. Agius, op. cit.

26 **St Francis of Assisi** (*c.* 1181–1226). *The Mirror of Perfection*, intro. by Hugh McKay and postscript by Eric Doyle (London, J. M. Dent, 1963).

27 **St Francis of Assisi** (*c.* 1181–1226). From G. and M. Harcourt (eds.), *Short Prayers for the Long Day* (London, Collins, 1978).

27 **St Anthony of Padua** (1195–1231). *The Mirror of Perfection* (London, J. M. Dent, 1963).

28 **St Catherine of Siena** (*c.* 1347–1380). 'Letters' cited in A. Agius, op. cit.

29 **Julian of Norwich** (*c.* 1360–?). *Showings*, tr. and intro. by Edmund Colledge and James Walsh, Classics of Western Spirituality (London, SPCK, 1979).

28 **Samuel Taylor Coleridge** (1772–1834). From 'The Rime of the Ancient Mariner', part vii, in Peter Levi (ed.), *Penguin Book of Christian Verse* (Harmondsworth, Penguin Books, 1985).

28 **Robert Browning** (1812–1899). From 'Saul' in *Poems of Robert Browning* (London and New York, Oxford University Press, 1911).

29 **Walt Whitman** (1819–1892). From 'Song of Myself' in *Whitman*, selected by Robert Creeley (Harmondsworth, Penguin Books, 1973).

29 **John Ruskin** (1819–1900). Speech to the Society for the Prevention of Cruelty to Animals, cited in Jon Wynne-Tyson (ed.), *The Extended Circle: A Dictionary of Human Thought* (Fontwell, Sussex, Centaur Press, 1985).

29 **Axel Munthe** (1857–1949). *The Story of San Michele* (London, John Murray, 1948). Our thanks to Ros Hirst for this reference.

30 **William Ralph Inge** (1860–1954). 'The Rights of Animals' in *Lay Thoughts of a Dean* (New York and London, The Knickerbocker Press, 1926).

30 **Albert Schweitzer** (1875–1965). *My Life and Thought*, tr. C. T. Campion (London, Allen and Unwin, 1933).

31 **C. S. Lewis** (1898–1963). 'Vivisection', first published as a pamphlet by the New England Anti-Vivisection Society 1947 and reproduced in *Undeceptions: Essays on Theology and Ethics*, ed. by Walter Hooper (London, Geoffrey Bles, 1962).

31 **Jürgen Moltmann** (twentieth century). *God in Creation: An Ecological Doctrine of Creation*, tr. Margaret Kohl (London, SCM Press, 1985).

31 **Robert Graves** (1895–1986). 'In the Wilderness' in A. Methuen (ed.), *An Anthology of Modern Verse*, 4th edn. (London, Methuen, 1921).

32 **Sylvia Lynd** (twentieth century). From 'The Return of the Goldfinches' in A. Methuen (ed.), op. cit.

32 **Pope John Paul II** (1920–). Message on 'Reconciliation' delivered at Assisi, 12 March 1982, and printed in *L'Osservatore Romano* (29 March 1982).

34 **St Basil the Great** (c. 330–379). 'Petition' cited in Jon Wynne-Tyson (ed.), op. cit.

34 **John Galsworthy** (1867–1933). From Richard Newman (ed.), *Bless All Thy Creatures, Lord: Prayers for Animals* (London and New York, Macmillan, 1982).

35 **Teilhard de Chardin** (1881–1955). *Hymn of the Universe*, tr. Gerald Vann (London, Fontana, 1974).

35 **Penelope Fleming** (twentieth century). 'All Creatures Great and Small', copyright P. R. Fleming 1987.

36 **Carmen Bernos de Gasztold** (twentieth century). 'The Prayer of the Dog' in *Prayers from the Ark* (Harmondsworth, Penguin Books, 1962).

36 **Source unknown**.

37 **J. R. Worsdall**. From Richard Newman (ed.), op. cit.

38 **The Creation Harvest Service** (1987). World Wildlife Fund.

3 RESPONSIBILITY

43 **St Francis of Assisi** (c. 1181–1226). *The Mirror of Perfection*, intro. by Hugh McKay and postscript by Eric Doyle (London, J. M. Dent, 1963).

43 **John Calvin** (1509–1564). *Commentaries*, ed. and tr. J. Haroutunian with L. P. Smith, The Library of Christian Classics, vol. xxii (London, SCM Press, 1958).

44 **George Fox** (1624–1691). *Doctrinal Books*, vol. i, 1831/1975 edn., and extract in Chris Lawson (ed.), *Some Quaker Thoughts on Animal Welfare* (London, Quaker Social Responsibility and Education, 1985).

44 **Thomas Traherne** (1637–1674). *Centuries: The Third Century*, para. 74 (Leighton Buzzard, The Faith Press, 1960).

44 **Alexander Pope** (1688–1744). 'Of Cruelty to Animals' in Rosalind Vallance (ed.), *A Hundred English Essays* (London, Thomas Nelson, 1950).

45 **John Woolman** (1720–1772). *Journal*, ed. by Moulton and cited in Chris Lawson (ed.), op. cit.

45 **William Cowper** (1731–1800). From 'Winter Walk at Noon' in R. A. Wilmott (ed.), *Poetical Works* (London, Routledge and Sons, 1854).

45 **William Blake** (1757–1827). From 'Auguries of Innocence' in Peter Levi (ed.), *Penguin Book of Christian Verse* (Harmondsworth, Penguin Books, 1985).

47 **Lord Shaftesbury** (1801–1885). Speech on the second reading of the Cruelty to Animals Bill, 26 May 1876, cited in Jon Wynne-Tyson (ed.), *The Extended Circle: A Dictionary of Humane Thought* (Fontwell, Sussex, Centaur Press, 1985).

47 **Cardinal Manning** (1808–1892). Speech to the Victoria Street Society for the Protection of Animals from Vivisection, 9 March 1887, printed in *Speeches against Vivisection* (London, Catholic Study Circle for Animal Welfare, no date).

47 **Cardinal Hinsley** (1865–1943). From a sermon, 1889, in Jon Wynne-Tyson (ed.), op. cit.

48 **Ella Wheeler Wilcox** (1850–1919). From 'Kinship' in Jon Wynne-Tyson (ed.), op.cit.

48 **Francis Brett Young** (1884–1954). From 'Bête Humaine' in J. C. Squire (ed.), *Selections from Modern Poets* (London, Martin Secker, 1926).

49 **Albert Schweitzer** (1875–1965). 'The Ethics of Reverence for Life' in *Christendom*, vol. i, no. 2 (New York 1952).

49 **Karl Barth** (1886–1968). *Church Dogmatics*, vol. iii *The Doctrine of Creation*, part 4, ed. by G. W. Bromiley and T. F. Torrance (Edinburgh, T. & T. Clark, 1961).

50 **Thomas Merton** (1915–1968). 'Unlived Life: A Manifesto against Factory Farming' (Campaigners against Factory Farming, 1966).

50 **E. F. Schumacher** (1911–1977). *Small is Beautiful: A Study of Economics as if People Mattered* (London, Abacus Press, 1974).

51 **Cardinal Heenan** (1905–1975). Foreword to A. Agius, *God's Animals* (London, Catholic Study Circle for Animal Welfare, 1970).

52 **Donald Coggan** (1909–). Presidential message to the Annual General Meeting of the RSPCA, printed in *RSPCA Today*, no. 22 (July 1977).

52 **John Austin Baker** (1928–). Sermon preached in York Minster, 28 September 1986, printed by Animal Christian Concern 1986.

53 **Jacob Boehme** (1575–1625). *The Way to Christ*, ed. and tr. Peter Erbs (SPCK/Paulist Press, 1979).

54 **George Matheson**. From Richard Newman (ed.), *Bless All Thy Creatures, Lord: Prayers for Animals* (London and New York, Macmillan, 1982).

54 **Richard Tatlock** (twentieth century). From Richard Tatlock (ed.), *A Book of Prayers* (London, Cassell, 1963).

54 **Richard Newman** (twentieth century). 'For Laboratory Animals' in Richard Newman (ed.), op. cit.

55 **Source unknown.**

56 **Society of United Prayer for Animals.**

57 **The RSPCA Order of Service** (1987). A form of confession from An Order of Service for Animal Welfare and/or Blessing compiled and written by Andrew Linzey (RSPCA 1987).

58 **The RSPCA Order of Service** (1987). Closing prayers, ibid.

59 **The Animal Christian Concern Order of Service** (1987).

59 **A Litany for Animals** (1985). A responsive prayer for animals by Robert A. Everett from the Service for Animal Rights Sunday, 28 April 1985, at the Emanuel United Church of Christ, New Jersey.

4 COMPASSION

65 **St John Chrysostom** (c. 347–407). Cited in Donald Attwater, *St John Chrysostom* (London, Catholic Book Club, 1960).

65 **St Isaac the Syrian** (c. 345–438). Cited in Vladimir Lossky, *The Mystical Theology of the Eastern Church* (Cambridge, James Clarke, 1952).

66 **St Richard of Chichester** (1197–1253). Cited in Butler's *Lives of the Saints* and in A. Agius, *God's Animals* (London, Catholic Study Circle for Animal Welfare, 1970).

66 **William Cowper** (1731–1800). From 'The Task' in R. A. Wilmott (ed.), *Poetical Works* (London, Routledge and Sons, 1854).

67 **William Blake** (1757–1827). 'On Another's Sorrow', from *Songs of Innocence and of Experience* in *Complete Poems* (London, Penguin, 1977).

68 **Humphry Primatt** (eighteenth century). *The Duty of Mercy and the Sin of Cruelty* (Edinburgh, Constable, 1834).

68 **Cardinal Newman** (1801–1890). Cited in Maisie Ward, *Young Mr Newman* and in A. Agius, op. cit.

68 **Henry Wadsworth Longfellow** (1807–1882). From 'The Birds of Killingworth' in *Poetical Works* (London and New York, Oxford University Press, 1917).

69 **Thomas Hardy** (1840–1928). From 'The Blinded Bird' in *The Complete Poems*, ed. by James Gibson, The New Wessex Edition (London, Macmillan, 1976).

69 **James Stephens** (1882–1950). 'The Snare' in A. Methuen (ed.), *An Anthology of Modern Verse*, 4th edn. (London, Methuen, 1921).

70 **Edith Sitwell** (1887–1964). From 'Still Falls the Rain' in Peter Levi (ed.), *The Penguin Book of Christian Verse* (Harmondsworth, Penguin Books, 1985).

70 **Thomas Hardy** (1840–1928). From 'Compassion: An Ode in Celebration of the Centenary of the Royal Society for the Prevention of Cruelty to Animals', 22 January 1924, ibid.

70 **Albert Schweitzer** (1875–1965). *Civilization and Ethics*, tr. C. T. Campion (London, Unwin Books, 1967).

71 **Tiruvalluvan** (ninth century). From Jon Wynne-Tyson (ed.), *The Extended Circle: A Dictionary of Humane Thought* (Fontwell, Sussex, Centaur Press, 1985).

71 **Archbishop Carter of Cape Town** (1850–1941). Composed in 1929, cited in C. W. Hume, *The Status of Animals in the Christian Religion* (London, Universities Federation for Animal Welfare, 1957).

71 **Rodborough Bede Book**. From Richard Newman (ed.), *Bless All Thy Creatures, Lord: Prayers for Animals* (London and New York, Macmillan, 1982).

72 **Liam Brophy**. 'Lamb of God' in Richard Newman (ed.), op. cit.

72 **Source unknown.**

73 **Source unknown.**

73 **From the Rituale Romanum.**

74 **Source unknown.**

74 **May Tripp** (twentieth century). Copyright 1986. The Prayer of Animal Christian Concern.

5 REDEMPTION

81 **Origen** (175–211). 'An Exhortation to Martyrdom' in *Origen*, tr. and intro. by Rowan A. Greer, Classics of Western Spirituality (London, SPCK, 1979).

81 **St Athanasius** (*c.* 296–373). *Ad Seraphionem*, 1.31, cited and discussed in T. F. Torrance, *Theology in Reconstruction* (London, SCM Press, 1965).

81 **St Gregory Nazianzen** (*c.* 330–389). From 'On the Son' in *Selected Poems*, tr. and intro. by John McGuckin (Oxford, SLG Press, 1986).

82 **St Cyril of Jerusalem** (*c.* 380–444). Cat. 16.1 and 40.16, cited and discussed in T. F. Torrance, op. cit.

82 **St John of the Cross** (1542–1591). *The Complete Works of St John of the Cross*, ed. and tr. by A. E. Peers, 3 vols. in one edn., vols. ii, v (Wheathampstead, Hertfordshire, Anthony Clarke, 1974).

83 **John Donne** (1572–1631). 'Holy Sonnets, XII' in *Complete Poetry and Selected Prose*, ed. by John Hayward (London, None-such Press, 1978).

83 **Robert Southey** (1774–1843). 'On the Death of a Favourite Spaniel', cited in J. G. Woods, *Man and Beast: Here and Hereafter*, 8th edn. (London, Gibbings and Co., 1903).

84 **John Wesley** (1703–1791). 'The General Deliverance' in *Sermons on Several Occasions*, vol. ii (London, Wesleyan Conference Office, 1874).

84 **F. D. Maurice** (1805–1872). 'Suffering and Glory' in *Sermons Preached in Country Churches*, 2nd edn. (London, Macmillan, 1880).

84 **F. D. Maurice** (1805–1872). 'Man's Dominion', ibid.

85 **Alfred Lord Tennyson** (1809–1892). 'In Memoriam' in *The Works* (London, Macmillan, 1889).

85 **Vladimir Lossky** (1903–1958). *The Mystical Theology of the Eastern Church* (Cambridge, James Clarke, 1973).

85 **Dietrich Bonhoeffer** (1906–1945). *Christology*, tr. John Bowden, intro. by E. H. Robertson (London, Fontana, 1966).

86 **The Byzantine Rite** (1978). Verse from the Mattins of Holy Saturday in The Lenten Triodion, tr. Mother Mary and Archimandrite Kallistos Ware (London, Faber and Faber, 1978), cited and discussed in A. M. Allchin, *The Dynamic of Tradition* (London, Darton, Longman and Todd, 1981).

86 **St Basil the Great** (*c.* 330–379). Attributed to St Basil in Richard Newman (ed.), *Bless All Thy Creatures, Lord: Prayers for Animals* (London and New York, Macmillan, 1982).

87 **Henry Vaughan** (1622–1695). From 'The Book' in *Silex Scintillans*, 1655, cited in Stephen R. L. Clark, *The Moral Status of Animals* (Oxford, Clarendon Press, 1977).

87 **A Christian's Prayer Book** (1973). From Peter Coughlan, Ronald C. D. Jasper and Teresa Rodrigues OSB (eds.), *A Christian's Prayer Book: Psalms, Poems and Prayers for the Church's Year* (London, Geoffrey Chapman, 1973).

88 **The RSPCA Order of Service** (1987). From An Order of Service for Animal Welfare and/or Blessing, compiled and written by Andrew Linzey (RSPCA 1987).

88 **The RSPCA Order of Service** (1987). A form of blessing, ibid.

88 **The RSPCA Order of Service** (1987). A form of absolution, ibid.

89 **The RSPCA Order of Service** (1987). Closing prayers, ibid.

89 **May Tripp** (twentieth century). Copyright 1986. The Animal Christian Concern 'Alpha and Omega' Prayer.

Also published by SPCK

CHRISTIANITY AND THE RIGHTS OF ANIMALS
Andrew Linzey

'. . . one of the most important contributions to understanding the relationship between humankind and animals that has yet appeared.' *Church Times*

'. . . a stimulating, well-reasoned and thoroughly convincing book.' *Church of England Newspaper*

'. . . simply the best book that I have ever read on Christianity and animal rights. Writing with great clarity he discusses every one of the animal rights issues from a profoundly Christian point of view.'
International Society for Animal Rights Report

'Whilst it is addressed primarily to those of the Christian tradition I would recommend his book to all who have an interest in animals, for the arguments advanced against specific cruelties are so well presented that they can be used by those of any faith, or none.' *International Animal Action*

'. . . a theological *tour de force* for the animal world.'
The Animals' Agenda

'This is a fair, honest, readable book . . . It avoids bigotry, extremism, self-righteousness and sentimentality, and asks its readers to do the same. I warmly commend it.' *Reform*

'. . . essential reading for anyone who wishes to look deeper into Christian thinking on animals.' *The Friend*

Christianity and the Rights of Animals is available from bookshops, or from the Mail Order Department, SPCK, Holy Trinity Church, Marylebone Road, London NW1 4DU. Price: £5.95 net (plus p & p).

The North American edition is published by the Crossroad/Continuum Publishing Co., 370 Lexington Avenue, New York, NY 10017. Price: $12.95.

PRAYERS FOR PEACE

An anthology of readings and prayers
selected by Archbishop Robert Runcie
and Cardinal Basil Hume.

'Inspiring words from the world's greatest saints and
religious thinkers intermingle with telling phrases from
more ordinary writers caught up in the struggle for peace.'
Church Times

'It would be difficult to imagine a more representative selec-
tion of readings, poems and prayers . . . and the comprehensive *Publisher's Notes on Sources* is exceptionally useful.'
The Inquirer

'This book is a gold mine for individuals and groups.'
The Universe

'. . . an anthology to be dipped into and used for prayer or
reflection.'
The Way

'. . . full of insights.' *Church of England Newspaper*

'. . . not to be missed.' *Expository Times*

Prayers for Peace is available from bookshops, or from
the Mail Order Department, SPCK, Holy Trinity
Church, Marylebone Road, London NW1 4DU.
Price £2.50 net (plus p & p).

All royalties donated to
Amnesty International